Caldaro da sei some

Caldaro da 4 some

Forno di rame có li trepiedi

Conserua mezana

Conserua dele grandi

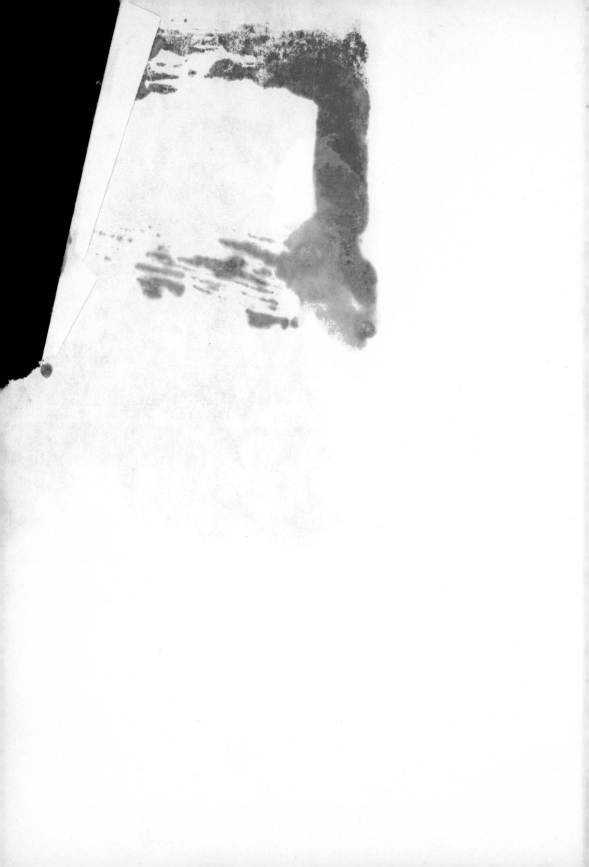

COOKING AND EATING

COOKING
AND
EATING

A PICTORIAL HISTORY
WITH RECIPES

KATIE STEWART

in collaboration with
Pamela and Maurice Michael

HART-DAVIS, MACGIBBON

© Pamela & Maurice Michael 1975

First published in Great Britain in 1975
by Hart-Davis, MacGibbon Ltd.,
Frogmore, St Albans, Hertfordshire, AL2 2NF
and 3 Upper James Street, London, W1R 4BP

ISBN 0 246 10829 0

Printed in Great Britain by Jarrold & Sons Ltd, Norwich

Contents

ACKNOWLEDGEMENTS

The authors and publishers of this book wish to record their gratitude to the staffs of the British Library, British Museum, London Library, and Nordiska Museet, Stockholm, and to the librarians of the Royal Asiatic Society for all their help, and to the following institutions and persons for permission to reproduce works in their possession.

Musée Arlatien
Bibliothèque de l'Arsenal, Paris
Bibliothèque Royale Albert Ier, Bruxelles
Biblioteca Nacional, Madrid
Trustees of the British Museum
Öffentliche Kunstsammlung Basel
Staatliche Museen zu Berlin
Bodleian Library, Oxford
Bibliothèque Royale de Belgique,
    Bruxelles
Bibliothèque Nationale, Paris
Museum Boymans-van Beunigngen,
    Rotterdam
Musée des Beaux-Arts, Strasbourg
The Chester Beatty Library
Musée Condé
Christ Church, Oxford
Gabinetto Fotografico Nazionale, Rome
Glenbow-Alberta Institute
Colourphoto Hans Hinz
India Office Library
Rijksmuseum G.M. Kam, Nijmegen
Musée du Louvre
Mr Hans Lidman, Sweden
Museen für Kunst und Kulturgeschichte
    der Hansestadt Lübeck
Rijksmuseum van Oudheden, Leiden
Museo Mandralisca, Afalu
Minnesota Historical Society

Coll. Molinar Pradelli, Bologna
Museo Archeologico Nazionale, Naples
National Gallery, London
Nordiska Museet, Stockholm
Preservation Society of Newport County
Oesterreichische Nationalbibliothek,
    Vienna
Oklahoma Historical Society
Oregon Historical Society
The Historical Society of Pennsylvania
Pergamon Museum, Berlin
Rheinisches Landesmuseum, Trier
Römische Germanisches Museum
Stiftsbibliothek St Gallen
Bibliothek de San Marco, Venice
Science Museum, London
Amministrazione Principe Torlonia
Metropolitan Toronto Central Library
Fototeca del Vaticano
Valentine Museum, Virginia
Vancouver Public Library
University Library, Istanbul
Universitetets Oldsaksamling, Oslo
Württembergerisches Landesmuseum,
    Stuttgart
The Colonial Williamsburg Foundation
University of Glasgow Hunterian
    Museum

Introduction

The proof of the pudding is traditionally in the eating. But I suppose I had been too busy cooking to wonder much about the ways in which people ate. That was until the idea of this book was suggested to me. Then it suddenly seemed the obvious thing to combine the two and write about cooking *and* eating. The moment we started work it became obvious that to write a proper history of this vast subject would have called for years of study and the knowledge of eight or nine languages, so we compromised on a pictorial history and we hope that its sequence of pictures and the relatively short text will provide an interesting introduction to the story of how people have cooked, what they have eaten and how they have eaten what they have cooked.

In the writing of this book I have learnt many things and had several false impressions corrected. I have looked at food and the cooking of it from Roman and medieval times right up to the nineteenth century. I have been intrigued to see how often in the past the male historian who did not cook has given a false picture of the cuisine of his period. Perhaps because the translator of his sources has not been sufficiently interested (one supposes) to ferret out the correct meaning of the unfamiliar word when his dictionary only gave him a generic term. I have also realized how many of us, myself included, have jumped to easy conclusions such as the familiar idea that the variety of spices used meant that the meat being cooked was tainted and so the taste had to be disguised. In the past many writers have pronounced medieval cooking as dull and monotonous, whereas in fact they had a longer list of fish and birds on their menus than we see today. They used a greater variety of spices and cooked their foods in just as many ways. Not only that, they used many more parts of the animals they slaughtered than we do. Indeed, as far as variety is concerned, the boot is on the other foot. We may have fish fingers but they had lampreys and many other delicious things.

Religion has had a surprising effect on what people ate. In Christendom it decreed meatless days, so greatly increasing the consumption of fish. In the Near and Far East, the rules of good hygiene were incorporated in religion and this barred the use, for instance, of pig and scaled fish to millions of people, while the laws of Islam, and in particular the Hindu, provided strict rules governing the manner of eating the dishes prepared.

The plentiful, or otherwise, supply of fuel affected the way people cooked. In Europe we have never really been short of fuel because of the discovery, before our wood supplies ran out, first of coal and then of gas and electricity. But in ancient civilizations whose people cut down the trees and where soil erosion ate into the land, fuel, that is to say wood, became scarce and expensive 2,000 or more years ago, so people learnt to cook on small fires, often cutting the food small so that it would cook more quickly.

The whole philosophy of cooking, that is the desire to achieve the most nutritious and savoury result by combining and contrasting textures, tastes, smells and visual appearance, proves to be basically the same the world over, though the results can be superficially very different. Perhaps what has surprised me most is the discovery of how well people ate in the past and how imaginative they were. Many of the dishes of Rome, medieval and Renaissance Europe, as well as of the Near and Far East are superb by any standards and that is why we have included a selection of the best in a separate Cook's Section.

The search for these recipes has been fascinating and very rewarding. So many to pick from – but I have chosen only those which are practical to cook these days and ones with ingredients that can be obtained without difficulty. I tested many recipes but included only those which are memorable. Today's cooks will be intrigued with the lovely sauces, the combinations of herbs and spices and the unusual flavours that they offer. A unique collection of recipes that are quite different and delicious. I have had to guess a little when the instructions were vague but I have stuck to the originals as closely as possible and the recipes have not lost any of their charm for having been brought up to date. I am indebted to Kenneth Lo, friend, colleague and well-known authority on Chinese food, for his selection of old Chinese recipes. They are delightful to read and give a charming insight into life in ancient China.

The recipes are grouped together in sections: Roman, Medieval, German and Italian seventeenth century, Chinese, Persian and Indian, American and eighteenth- to nineteenth-century English. Each one includes a limited variety of soups, main dishes, vegetable recipes and puddings. One can choose recipes from any section to make up a menu. If after you have invited your friends to a Roman dinner and given them *porcellum aenococtum*, or an eighteenth-century meal and served our syllabub, they don't ask to borrow this book or write down the recipe I shall be very surprised.

Of all the books I have been involved in this one has given me the greatest satisfaction. Work on the book provided interesting sidelights on the art of carving and the importance of presentation and theories of diet and health, among other things. It has extended my knowledge of a past way of life. If it gives you as much pleasure to read this book as it gave me to work on it, I shall consider the task well done.

Assurbanipal celebrating a victory by dining with his queen and officers while musicians play and the head of his vanquished enemy glowers from the branch on which it has been impaled.

Ancient Times

Among primitive peoples it would seem that cooking has always been the woman's job; but as soon as people became civilized and began to think of what they ate as a gift from the gods for which they should be grateful, a religious element entered into the preparation of food which then seems to have become the duty of men. Men have always sought to make the exercise of religion an all-male affair and, in the olden days especially, women were kept on the periphery of all such activities, except for fertility rights and minor roles as soothsayers and voices for oracles. And so it seems to have been with cooking, certainly where the preparation of the 'burned offerings', were concerned – those token sacrifices which purported to give the gods their 'share' of the food, but which were mere whiffs of glorious smells, while their priests and the people ate the food. In Homeric times, even kings were not above cooking their own meals, and, judging by the pictures of kitchen scenes and the models found in the tombs, the Egyptian cooks were all men, as were Greek and Roman cooks.

The normal fuel for cooking right up to the eighteenth century was charcoal or wood, except in the Arctic, where there is no wood. There the

Model of an Egyptian bread-oven.
The baker is holding a sort of trowel
for inserting the loaves and, perhaps,
also to fan the fire. His hand shields
his face from the heat.

Eskimoes used animals oils, which they burned using wicks made of moss arranged round the rim of a stone stove shaped like a ring mould. The fire to burn the fuel was obtained first by rubbing two pieces of wood together and, for the last several thousand years, by striking iron pyrites or steel with a piece of flint, the resulting sparks igniting a piece of tinder. This latter was the method that remained in use until the invention of the match in the nineteenth century.

The people of ancient Babylon cooked over an 'oven', presumably a covered stove, in the courtyard of their houses. The Egyptians had ovens in which they baked, but cooked mostly over an open fire, fanning the coals to maintain a regular heat. Only the Chinese had proper enclosed cooking-stoves in those early days. The Roman stove was raised and had a flat top upon which the fire was built. The Greeks appear to have cooked over open fires and baked on a flat surface with a fire underneath.

The Babylonians used a lot of barley both for food and drink. Their bread was unleavened. They added honey, ghee, sesame oil and milk to

To obtain extra heat the Egyptian cook fanned his fire which was built on a flat stone surface, as in this model.

flour to make pastry and cakes. They had onions, lentils, beans, peas, cucumber and cabbage and lettuce. They used dates as a source of sugar and made wine from them, and they ate the heart of the palm tree, which is not unlike celery, and to them was a delicacy. They grew apples, figs, quinces and pomegranates. They used the milk of sheep, goats and cows, mostly in the form of yoghurt or cheese. They ate a lot of fish, but beef, mutton or goat were more or less reserved for special occasions. They probably ate more pork than anything.

The Babylonians used knives and spoons made of bitumen or bone. They had earthenware ladles and bronze frying-pans. None of their recipes have survived, nor do we have any from Egypt; but we know that the Egyptians bred cattle, antelope, oryx, etc., for their meat, as well as goats and sheep. They probably ate mutton, but pork seems to have been forbidden, as were certain kinds of fish. They did not eat chickens, but lots of ducks, often artificially fattened, geese, quails and pigeons. They had no oranges, lemons or bananas, but leeks, onions, cucumber, garlic

The main item in the Greeks' diet was fish of all kinds from river trout to shellfish. Here is a fishmonger cutting up a tunny. Note the leaves in his hair to help keep away the flies.

and water-melons. Lettuce was sacred to the ithyphallic deity Min. They had grapes, figs, dates, olives, lotus fruits, pomegranates and apples. Milk to drink was a delicacy, but they used it to make cream, butter and cheese. They sweetened their food with carob seed and honey, bees being kept in most private gardens in pottery-jar hives.

When Piankhi, a king of Ethiopia, conquered Egypt, he refused to allow the princes of the South and of the Delta to eat at his table, because they were 'lechers and fish-eaters', as though the two were synonymous. The fish the Egyptians ate were mainly mullet, catfish and Nile perch, which were often dried in the sun and eaten raw, or salted. The Egyptians had eighteen different words for bread or cakes which were baked with flour made of barley, spelt and, latterly, wheat. They ground daily the exact quantity of flour required for that day's consumption. They knew and used leaven.

In their kitchens the Egyptians had two-handled saucepans of different depths, wide enough slightly to overlap the stove they rested on. They had portable cylindrical earthenware stoves about three feet high which had bars inside to bake loaves on. Boiling and grilling seem to have been their favourite methods.

The Egyptians had the animals they were to cook delivered to the kitchen ready butchered, that is drawn and skinned and, presumably, hung. They did not slaughter in the kitchen as was done in medieval Europe and indeed up to the seventeenth and even eighteenth century.

Eating habits have varied enormously. Among primitive peoples you find everything from the cosy circle gathered round the cooking-fire to the Australian Aboriginals sitting back to back so that neither could see what the other was eating or how. The Babylonians seem to have sat on chairs or stools. The Egyptians ate singly or in pairs at small tables, with the children sitting on cushions on the floor. Breakfast was not a family meal, but a breaking of the night's fast in solitude. They had spoons and probably forks, but ate mostly with their fingers. At banquets the host and privileged guests were seated on high-backed seats, the rest sat on cross- or straight-legged stools. Men and women usually sat on opposite sides of the room, but sometimes they mixed, and then husband and wife could sit together. In the late period, towards the end of the meal a model of a mummified corpse and coffin, carved and painted with great care, would be carried round and shown to the guests to remind them of the joys of living and the miseries of the Kingdom of the Dead. 'Look on this', they were told, 'and then drink and take your pleasure, for when you are

All cooking was with oil. Here an oil-merchant is serving a customer.

dead thus will you be.' A custom, one would have thought, calculated to put a damper on any party.

The Greeks of Homer put their gods on a monotonous diet of nectar and ambrosia, but they did better for themselves. They ate very simply and kings were not above cooking their own food. In Homeric times everybody was supposed to get the same-sized helping.

Homer called salt 'divine' and in one passage in the *Odyssey* he speaks disparagingly of 'islanders who do not know the sea and use no salt in their food'. The fact is, of course, that people who live mainly on milk and flesh which they eat raw, or roasted, have no need to add sodium chloride to their food, for roast meat retains its salts, but those whose diet is cooked cereals and vegetables do need to add it. Whether the Greeks were aware of this, the Romans certainly were, for in the early days the officers and men of the Roman Army were given an allowance of salt. This was later converted into a cash allowance called a *salarium*, from which comes our word 'salary'.

The ancient Greek breakfast and lunch were summary affairs, but dinner was a good spread of several courses. You did not drink during meals, only at the end with dessert.

Greek cooking was mostly grilling and roasting. Nobody cooked unnecessarily because of the labour of lighting and making a fire of the necessary size and heat. Thus take-home meals were a common feature

Sugar was unknown and the only sweetening was honey which was gathered with considerably greater difficulty than is the case today.

Take-away meals are no modern invention, but a common feature of life in ancient Greece, where few were wealthy enough to afford a (slave) chef of their own. Hot courses could be bought at stalls like this and for parties you could always hire a chef to come in and do the cooking for you.

of urban life, being bought from stalls that mostly were simple affairs like that modelled here. Shops sold fish, fruit, and the oil that was universally used for cooking, butter being rare and reserved for certain religious rites. Honey was the only sweetener.

Homeric Greeks sat to eat, the later and more luxurious Athenians reclined, adopting the lazy way which the Babylonians started about the seventh century B.C.

We don't know much about Greek family meals except that fish (tunny, mackerel, whitebait, mullet and – a delicacy – eel), fruit, bread and oil were the main ingredients; and that when they ate meat it was either game, poultry or pork, beef and mutton being eaten only on religious occasions. But we know practically everything about the Greek banquet. This was an all-male affair (except for the girls hired to amuse and entertain) and mostly held in a private house. When a guest arrived, he took off his shoes or sandals (they are often depicted under the couches) and slaves washed his feet and handed him a bowl of water in which to wash his hands. He then took his place on a couch for either one or two with a striped pillow to recline on and a low table standing beside it, on which his food was placed. After the meal the party proper began; that

17

Obviously the Greek family normally ate together, but the banquet or special party was an all-male affair except for the servants who might be girls and, of course, the entertainers. Guests reclined on couches with a low table beside them that could be tucked underneath when not required (page 20).

is to say, the girls (and many of the guests) arrived and with them drinking started. Wine was always mixed with water, sometimes the brackish water of the Aegean. A not so popular alternative to girls and drinking was serious conversation and learned debate, for which Plato and his circle are famous.

The Greeks paid particular attention to food being served hot, and there are stories of gluttons dipping their hands into very hot water in order to harden their fingers and so get a start on the other guests. One even experimented with a tongue-guard to enable him to stand hotter food, but he just burned the roof of his mouth. There are many scenes of feasting depicted on ancient Greek pots, but only one shows a man using a knife, so it was mostly fingers they used. When you eat with your fingers alone, your food has to be in pieces small enough to make a convenient mouthful or to be pressed together to make a ball of the right size. A

18

thick sauce that will help you make little balls is an advantage, but a runny gravy that cannot be mopped up is merely an embarrassment, however delicious – think of the problem of the melted butter when eating asparagus– and this was to remain a decisive factor that governed the type of food people ate as long as they reclined. Once they began to sit at table and to use spoons to convey the food to their mouths, they were able to eat a larger variety of foods.

It was in the fifth century that fine cooking came to Athens from Sicily along with Sicilian cooks, who were all men. Few Greeks were rich enough to afford a chef of their own and most people just hired them for special occasions. Good chefs were choosy and many wanted to see a list of the guests before accepting an engagement. These Sicilian cooks had their own cook-books, but none of them have survived. The accounts of feasts and entertainments in Athenaeus' *The Deipnosophists* give us a good idea of what was eaten, though only a rough idea of how it was prepared, sometimes no more than 'I took a widowed amia and plunged it like a living torch in the embers' which is poetry, but no recipe. Good quality and simplicity seem to have been the main characteristics, plus those qualities that come from slow cooking. When the Greek cook needed quick extra heat he would pour a little oil on the fire.

The Athenians and Romans had special dining-rooms called *triclinia*. These were furnished with anything from three to nine or more couches, double or single. The Greeks had a low table beside each couch, while the Roman couches were arranged in a 'U' round a large table. Although the Greeks couches, at least the single ones, had low backs against which a cushion was placed, so that if necessary the occupant could use both

A plate of figs recovered from an Egyptian tomb.

hands, the Romans seem to have been propped up on one elbow all the time. This restricted the type of food that could be served and meant that meat especially had to be presented in conveniently sized pieces, and this in turn meant that carving was of great importance. Indeed, the Romans regarded it as an art. They ran schools at which young men were taught it, practising on wooden models of all the joints, birds, game, etc., they were likely to encounter. These models were made up of ideally shaped pieces fixed together with string, or even glued.

At banquets a guest might be shown a menu so that he should know in advance the dishes he wanted to go for. Apparently the Greeks did not have napkins, but the Romans certainly did. You took one with you when you went out to dinner and sometimes used it to carry home delicious left-overs. Many Romans also took a light toga to put on when they reached the house where they were to dine.

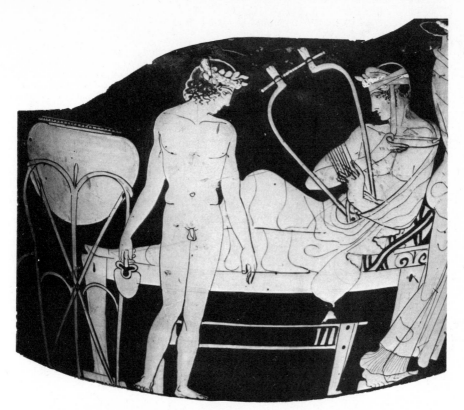

The Greeks (and the Romans) mixed their wine with water to make it taste less vinegary. The mixing was done in great bowls, from which it was served to the guests with jugs like this filled by dipping into the bowl. The cup was a shallow saucer shape like that opposite.

In the second half of Greek parties drinking was fairly heavy and the call for a slave to 'bring a pot' was anything but unusual. (In this respect the Greek reveller was one up on the eighteenth-century two-bottle man who had himself to fetch his pot from the sideboard.) These pots (with their contents) were on occasion used as missiles.

The Greeks were very concerned about the medicinal properties of the foods they ate and carefully noted whether they were diuretic, laxative, costive, good for the heart, brain, bowels, etc., and so people did for the next 1,500 years or more. One suspects that sometimes menus were dictated more by the needs of bowel discipline than by the rules of gastronomy. Perhaps the Greek or Roman hostess kept a card index of her guests' ailments, as hostesses today do of their friends' likes and dislikes.

Animal foods were held to nourish, fatten and strengthen above all

A Roman colander.

Opposite: a vessel for carrying and pouring liquids at table.

other foods, but they tended to make you very full-blooded, especially if you drank wine with your meal. Mutton was considered especially heating and so unsuitable for those of a feverish or choleric temperament. Carrot was held to impart 'pungency' to the sperma and increase the flow of urine. Some also thought that it assisted coition and stimulated the menses, but on the other hand it generated unhealthy blood. Cabbage was a specific against intoxication and hangover, as was saffron water drunk before taking wine. Lettuce was thought to be (*a*) a good regulatory and soporific and to check sexual desire, and (*b*) to increase the flow of sperma. Cooked turnip was a cure for cold feet.

These beliefs showed that they were fumbling towards scientific nutrition and a balanced diet; though they did not get very far.

Before they came under Greek influence the Romans had looked upon cooking as a servile task. After the Rape of the Sabines, the companions of Romulus and Remus, wishing to placate the rest of the people, promised to free them from the chores of making bread and preparing meals. However, once they came under the influence of the Greeks, they soon changed their attitude.

When we think of Roman eating, what we remember is the tales of the *vomitorium* and of dishes of nightingales' tongues, etc., with which Latin masters used to try to make their lessons interesting. Such things, of course, did exist, but they were the extravagances of the ostentatious *nouveaux riches* of the late Empire, the Roman equivalent of the Edwardian beau drinking pink champagne out of a girl's slipper; a good story, but quite untypical. But the cuisine of the Roman Empire was the first truly cosmopolitan one.

The Roman broke his fast with bread dipped in wine and, perhaps,

22

some onions and cheese, probably made of sheep or goat's milk. At 11 am or noon he would have bread and fruit and, perhaps, more cheese, with water to wash it down. His main meal was in the evening, about 5 or 6 pm. The richer he was, the later the time of his evening meal. In all civilizations people have tended to get up later and eat later, the more 'civilized' or leisured they became.

Roman cooking was quite advanced. They cooked in oil. Their stoves were raised and their cauldrons – covered pots, pans, etc. – of which they had a variety were mostly set on low iron tripods over a charcoal or wood fire. Judging by Apicius' recipes, they roasted a lot. Obviously they roasted on spits, but they must also have roasted in ovens or metal roasting dishes like those we use today. They had two sorts of oven, a larger one

23

Roman housewife selecting a goose at the poulterer's.

A Greek dish depicting some of the fish that were eaten.

An Egyptian serving-dish, showing fish.

Another Egyptian serving-dish.

Some delicious-looking duck served 4,000 years ago and found, desiccated, in an ancient tomb.

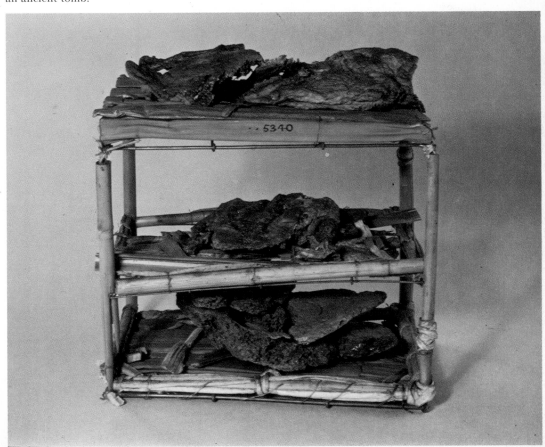

where the fire was made inside the oven and the ashes raked out when the right heat had been obtained, as was the system for the next 1,000 years, and a smaller oven with double walls. Here the fire was built underneath with the flames going up and round the inner wall heating the space inside, almost exactly the principle of Count Rumford's invention of the 1780s.

A seemingly inevitable ingredient of every Roman dish was *garum*, a liquid flavouring made from brine and fish which had been adapted from the Greek γαρον and which they used almost as liquid salt. It was mass-produced in factories and few people made their own. People now think that one can satisfactorily reconstitute *garum* and one can see that as well as a flavouring, it was a condiment. Indeed, it may well be true that food is better flavoured if you use a liquid, rather than a dry salt.

The Romans had a rich variety of sauces and at their main meals must have eaten with spoons as much as with their fingers. They also used hardwood sticks, like single chopsticks for eating meat.

When the Romans cooked in wine, they first reduced the wine before adding it to what they were cooking, as we still do to drive off the alcohol and leave the wine taste. They had a wine-based sweet sauce called *passum*, which was made from dried grapes pounded in old or fresh wine.

Roman marinades were of specially prepared wine, vinegar, honey, brine, pepper, herbs and spices. Latterly they pretended to dislike the

Above: A Roman jug.

Below: A Roman kitchen, bakery and buttery.

Left: Roman salt or condiment strewer.

Below: Roman frying pan

Right: A Roman cista, similar to the Victorian silver biscuit-box.

Centre: A Swedish *munkpanna* (doughnut-pan) which can still be found in country districts.

Below: A Roman pan of identical design and probably used for the same purpose.

Above: A dish of eggs from Pompeii.
Below: A gravy-spoon.

taste and texture of plain meat. Those were the days when they were said to have liked 'soft, voluptuous food' and 'sauces with a seductive feel that caressed the mouth'.

Their dinners could be quite elaborate and substantial, consisting of *hors d'œuvres* or entrée (*gustum gustatio*) accompanied by eggs done in a variety of ways and all sorts of vegetables cooked and raw, mushrooms, salt fish, oysters, mussels, snails and even dormice. Then came the main course (*mensa prima*) of meats and poultry, wine being drunk with this course. Then followed the dessert: fruits, sweets and, in classical times, savouries.

In the Roman dining-room, the host reclined in the middle of the 'U' of couches flanked by one or more guests of honour; then came the hostess and perhaps a woman relative, making a total of nine or possibly fewer. Each course was set on a table which was then carried in and inserted into

Food was kept hot on a special table-top chafing-dish made either of bronze or, as this one, of earthenware. They were called thermospodii.

33

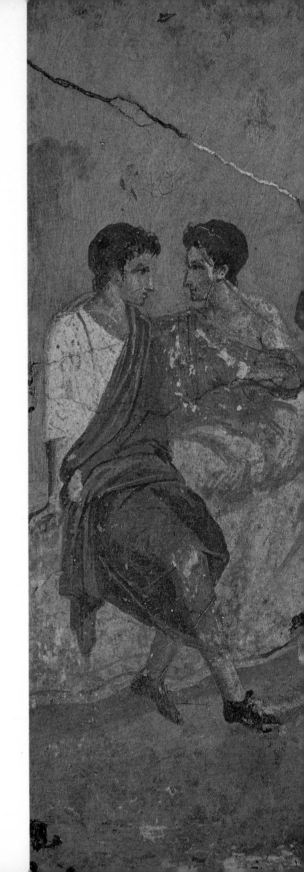

Banqueting scene from a fresco
found at Pompeii. A guest newly
arrived is having his shoes
removed by a servant while
another hands him a cup of wine.

the open end of the 'U'. When the diners had finished that particular course, the table was withdrawn and another with the next course ready laid on it, inserted in its place. Wine was served from behind each diner.

The diners would have finished eating by about 8 pm. If they were entertaining, the wife and any other women of the family would now withdraw and musicians, courtesans and probably a few hangers-on join the party, which then changed character radically.

The Romans had quite an impressive *batterie de cuisine*, part of which is illustrated here: bronze frying-pans, cauldrons, scoops, ladles, strainers, colanders, etc. – even fish-kettles with holes low down in the sides of the inner container through which a head or tail could, if necessary, be

The embossed lid of a serving-dish with figures of sucking-pig and various roast birds.

Opposite: A Roman family at dinner. The man reclines, the woman is seated at the end of the couch; the children await their turn.

pushed to allow the fish to lie flat. They had a sort of cake-pan with four or more depressions like an egg-poacher and of exactly the same design as the old Scandinavian *munkpanna* or doughnut pan made of stone, cast-iron or copper and which is still being made.

There was no cow's milk, for cows were beasts of burden and had only enough milk for their calves, so for cooking the Romans used sheep's or goat's milk. As in Egypt or Greece, large animals were only slaughtered in conjunction with religious occasions; so that the main flesh was poultry, pork or game. Hare was a favourite dish. The Romans did not eat horsemeat, but wild asses were bred for food. Wild boar, bear's meat, venison, wild sheep and wild goat which in those days were plentiful were

37

eaten, as was flamingo and stork. The Romans ate lots of fish: red mullet (the liver was a delicacy), mackerel, tunny and bonito, sardine, conger and brill, but fish was not easy to get in big cities because of the difficulty of keeping it. Both wild and domestic duck were eaten, and a lot of capons and geese.

Pheasants were farmed and so were peacocks and rabbits, from stock imported from Spain. Pigeons were kept for food and wild ones caught, and later puppies were eaten. The Romans knew all about forced feeding and how to smoke cheeses, and to some extent how to preserve food. They dried or otherwise preserved radishes, peaches, lemons, truffles, olives and quinces. Meat was salted and game drawn, stuffed with wheat or oats to absorb moisture and, still with its skin on, buried in flour or grain which again helped to dry it and keep it dry. As a result meat in the cities was usually tough and hard and sometimes had to be cooked twice; once in milk and once in water. This was, in fact, normal for hare, game and poultry.

From about 200 B.C. there were professional baker-millers who knew about fermentation. They had various ways of baking adding poppy-seed, aniseed, celery, fennel, sunflower, sesame, currants, etc., either to flavour the dough or to decorate the loaf when it had been painted with egg. In all they made several dozen kinds of bread. The Romans ate the eggs of hens (much smaller then), duck, pigeon, partridge and especially, geese,

Above: The Viking princess buried in the Oseberg ship was given these simple cooking implements to take with her on her last journey.

Below: A scene from the Bayeux Tapestry showing a large pot over an open fire, two cooks turning a spit mounted on two forked sticks; in the centre another cook is grilling meat and taking the ready pieces off the fire with a pair of tongs. To the right, a man holds two spitted birds that have been roasted whole.

Above: Here are some Romans at table with servants in the adjoining pantry. Note that the men are reclining, the women seated at the ends of the couches.

Opposite centre: Fish was an important part of the Roman diet. This famous mosaic gives an idea of the wide variety of types that were eaten. Meat and game were also much eaten, as was fruit, of which the Greeks too ate a lot.

Below right: A table laid with crockery and cutlery excavated at Roman sites.

Below: A Roman administrator of transalpine territories at dinner. He has his wife and children, and his dog beside him. Note the tablecloth. The round objects on the table could be apples, loaves or, perhaps, doughnuts made in the pan on page 31.

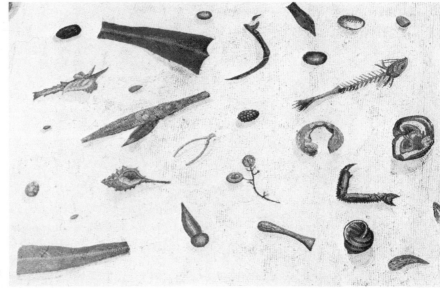

The Queen dines at a table on her own, the men being relegated to a side table under the windows of the hall. Note the buffet on the other side with its display of plate.

perhaps wild and sea-birds' eggs as well. Sweet omelettes were popular. You ate figs with bread. Grapes were ordinary fare. Bread was often dipped in oil, rubbed with garlic and eaten on its own. Apples were quartered and dried on trays, also stored in jars and barrels. Dried pears were considered a delicacy. Fruit was served as a main dish and included most of those we know and eat today. Green vegetables were often cooked with natron, a carbonate of soda, to preserve the colour. They did not think that this affected the flavour. As later in medieval times there was little or no waste, for almost every part of an animal was used, even palates and udders being considered delicacies. With our present shortages perhaps we ought to follow their example.

Like the Greeks, the Romans were particular about their food being served hot, and as Roman kitchens followed the tradition of being separate and somewhat apart from the rest of the house, they made use of charcoal stoves made of bronze or earthenware in which food could be reheated or kept hot, perhaps even cooked on the table. One of these discovered in Belgium proved to have a double liner in the upper compartment which suggests that it could have been used as a double-saucepan. When Rome and others of the big cities became uncomfortably overcrowded, many households in the makeshift flats, etc., had little or no means of cooking and had to buy most, if not all, their cooked food from stalls in the street and take it home to be eaten. Some did try to cook indoors on portable stoves and as a result there were frequent fires.

Officers or civil administrators serving in Gaul and elsewhere were better off. There was plenty of accommodation for them and the scene depicted on page 40 was no doubt typical: the man, an officer serving on the Rhine, with the dog beside him; and a small table with tablecloth and fruit, etc., on it; his wife sitting in the curved end of the sofa which is now only half a 'U'. They would appear to have lived well.

Medieval Cooking

According to Pliny, the Gauls and the Iberians, both drinkers of ale rather than wine, used the froth produced by brewing in baking their bread. This froth, which is where the yeast lives, was a better leaven than that used by the Greeks or Romans and as a result the Gauls and Iberians had lighter bread than other peoples. Although they had achieved this measure of competence, the collapse of the Roman Empire was as bad a setback to cooking as it was to the other arts. The destruction by the new masters of the former Romans' villas meant that people stopped using and soon forgot how to make the efficient flat-topped, Roman cooking-stove along with the other Roman aids to gracious living: central heating, water-closets and baths, to which incidentally the Romans always went before dining. People no longer took napkins when they went out to dinner, but licked their fingers instead. They were now back at the stage of cooking at open hearths with all their disadvantages of smoke and flying ash, to say nothing of the difficulties of stoking. It is easy enough to maintain a small fire over which a cauldron can simmer, or to make a hot fire at which to roast, but to make a fire at which both operations can be done is not easy. Even so, the recipes of the Romans must have been remembered, especially in Spain and the south of France where the Roman way of life was least disturbed.

Food and its preparation is the last thing people are likely to neglect. This is the area where man first begins to experiment once he has achieved a sufficiency and a little leisure. The real limitation on what people ate was the availability of other than the basic foods. The collapse of the Roman Empire brought the international exchange of goods to a full stop. Spices, larks' tongues and other delicacies were not only in short supply, but vanished from the shops. Suddenly people were compelled to make do with what could be obtained locally and it was to be hundreds of years before commerce really revived and with it the art of cooking. In those days kings were on occasion forced to issue edicts that no animal was to be slaughtered for food until it had produced offspring, and this meant that no lamb, kid or sucking-pig could appear on the menu. Often meat other than game or poultry and pigeons must have been scarce, and game itself was not necessarily always to be had. Normally people now ate meat only once a week, and this continued even after there were three meat days allowed in the week to the four meatless ones or 'fish days' on which you

45

One of the rare scenes of carving at table in the Middle Ages. Note the rectangular platters in front of the diners.

might eat only fish, eggs or porridges, provided that the days did not happen to be ember days or in Lent. The members of religious orders, which were among those best able to afford a good table, were not supposed to eat meat at all, but they were allowed it if they needed strengthening in sickness or convalescence; and it is surprising how many of the brethren were in that state. Meat was freely served to pilgrims and visitors, especially those of importance, and to the laity. Lent comes at the period of the year when food was hardest to come by; the winter's stores were dwindling or consumed, and Nature had not yet been able to replace them with anything new. It was a good time to make a virtue of necessity.

The ordinances of Charlemagne record that lettuces, cresses, endive, parsley, chervil, carrots, leeks, turnips, onions, garlic and 'escholots' were to be found nowhere but in the Emperor's kitchen gardens! Charlemagne seems to have gone into business as a nurseryman-seedsman and obtained a considerable revenue from selling from his gardens. Whether the monastery of St Gallen bought from him or had its own perhaps ecclesiastical, supplier, we do not know, but certainly when it was being planned at the beginning of the 800s not only was accommodation to be provided for sheep, cows and pigs, as well as for hens and geese, but there were to be extensive gardens and orchards, in which apple, pear, plum, sorb, medlar, bay, chestnut, fig, quince, peach, hazel, almond, mulberry and walnut trees were to be planted. The eighteen great beds of the

46

kitchen garden were to grow onions, leeks, celery, coriander, dill, poppy, raddish, carrots, mangold, garlic, shallots, parsley, chervil, lettuce, parsnip, cabbage and corn campion.

No mention was made of the horse- or fodder-bean, which St Gallen himself recommended for its health-giving properties. It had provided part of the daily fare of Rome's gladiators who ate it with barley-water, because it made the body fleshy and the flesh 'not firm and compact, as pork made it, but flabby'. (Presumably this was desirable only in gladiators.) Horse-bean meal was extensively used to cleanse the skin. It was what slave-dealers used to make their girl and boy wares look clean and attractive; and women also used it at the baths. Gallen says that its use removes liver-spots and freckles from the skin.

The monastery's kitchen garden plan shows how little green vegetables figured in people's diet in those days and for long to come. This was largely because they were thought to cause wind and induce melancholy, though the Romans had believed that cabbages were an excellent remedy for hangovers, an idea that persisted until well into the sixteenth century and beyond. At a banquet given by Catherine de Medici in 1549

A fourteenth-century scene. This looks horribly meagre fare.

artichoke hearts were the only vegetable served. Vegetable-growing as we know it only began in France during the reign of Henri IV (1589–1610) and in England not until the second half of the seventeenth century.

Wind seems to have been something of a social bugbear in early times. Although many Oriental peoples considered, and still consider, a good belch at the end of a meal as a welcome expression of appreciation, wind from the other quarter has always embarrassed. There is the heart-rending story of the rich young Persian merchant's son, Abu Hassan, who many years ago 'brake wind' at his own wedding feast and was so overcome with shame that he got up, walked out and away and was never seen again. To our twentieth-century way of thinking a fart seems a trivial reason for emigrating, but young Hassan felt that he had been guilty of a solecism that he could never live down, and so he had gone, abandoning a fortune and the bride he had never even seen.

Charlemagne's table is said to have been a long slab of oak in which hollows had been made at regular intervals. Your food was put straight into these hollows which acted as individual troughs and people ate from them – with both hands. They ate and drank immoderately and it was nothing unusual for people to be struck dead in a quarrel at table. In fact, the hopelessness of obtaining reliable witnesses from a group of drunken men feasting by the dim light of flickering torches was so well accepted that if more than seven persons were at the table no one was held responsible for such deaths.

Mutton is seldom mentioned as having been eaten in the early Middle Ages, probably because wool was then too valuable for sheep to be killed for food. Similarly beef was a rarity, because the value of cattle lay in their use as draught animals, while hides fetched more the older the animal they came from.

People ate with knives, pointed like hunting-knives, and later spoons, which they took about with them, but mainly with their own fingers. There is a miniature in an eleventh-century MS. at Monte Cassino (see page 57) which shows two men at table eating with forks, but this is unique. Forks were used at table in Byzantium and to a very limited extent in France during the early Middle Ages. An inventory made of Charles V's possessions in 1380 shows that he possessed a dozen forks, though we don't know whether or not they were used other than for carving. Charles of Savoy had only one fork 100 years later (1487). Mathius Corvinus, King of Hungary at the end of the fifteenth century, ate with his fingers as did Anne of Austria fifty years later. Henry IV of France was using a fork in the 1600s, but Louis XIV (1700) used his whole hand.

Today we find it difficult to see why it took so long for this fairly simple instrument to be generally adopted for table use. No doubt there were plenty of die-hards to assert – and rightly – that God made fingers before forks, but forks did help to keep your hand clean and to cut meat on your trencher or plate to pieces of suitable size. The fastidious Chinese had been using their equivalent, chopsticks, for 1,000 years before the average Englishman could handle a fork at table.

The London Pipe Roll of 1180 makes mention of a Guild of Pepperers; but pepper, which had been imported from the East into Alexandria and the Mediterranean in Roman times, was then a rarity and it did not become common in England until after 1500. Indeed, all spices were expensive, but pepper especially so and it was even left as a bequest in people's wills. Coming from the East, spices had a long way to travel, both in distance and time, so that when they came to be used they had probably lost a good deal of their pungency. One should thus be wary of using the quantities of spices indicated in some of the early books.

The kitchen was very much a place for the young.

Honey was still the main or only sweetener. Where wine was grown, 'must' or unfermented grape juice was also used. Sugar-cane was brought to Sicily some time before 1220 by a group of Jews from Maghreb (Morocco), but the earliest reference to its use in England is 1299. It was probably too difficult to get to be used by many until very much later; probably not until a Venetian discovered how to refine it in the late fifteenth century and the Spaniards began importing it from Madeira and America.

It was at this time, the turn of the thirteenth to fourteenth century, that Marco Polo returned to his native Italy after twenty-five years in China where he had been introduced to noodles and ravioli which the Chinese had already been making and eating for 1,000 years or more. Recent excavations at Turfan have shown that they were making the latter in A.D. 800 and no doubt long before, and it seems likely that Marco Polo taught the Italians how to make the two, and that this was the beginning of *pasta*. There are, of course, people who say that the Italians knew all about it long before Marco Polo's day, but there is no proof of that, while we do know that the Chinese had been making *pasta* for centuries before the Italian went there.

Salt of course, was all-important. Bay salt for preserving food, especially at the autumnal slaughtering of fat animals (there was no winter fodder for them in those days), and white salt for table use. The continental equivalent of the big silver container called 'the salt' was the nef, a silver model of a type of ship called a 'nef', the crow's-nest of which

A fourteenth-century woman stirring the pot, while one of her children plies the bellows.

At the medieval table (*above*) birds and fish were served whole. Knife and finger were the diner's only implements.

Spit-roasting. Note the dripping pan.

was a small container for salt (see page 74). This was usually kept locked to prevent poison being added to it. People of less or no importance were handed salt in a hollow in a piece of bread. Salt was obtained by evaporation (salt-pans) or by mining rock salt.

In the thirteenth century, the then King of Norway sought to teach his rude jarls and their sons some of the graces. Among his recommendations is the rather surprising one that at table (that is to say when dining with their king) they should speak in a tone so low that not a single word could be heard by those sitting on either side of the two who were conversing. The young Scandinavian was allowed 'to partake freely and quickly of both the food and the drink according to your needs without suffering any discredit to your manners'.

Four hundred years later the Rev. Trusler, a self-styled arbiter of good manners, was telling his readers the reverse: 'Eating quick or very slow at meals, is characteristic of the vulgar: the first infers poverty, that you have not had a good meal for some time; the last, if abroad, that you dislike your entertainment; if at home, that you are rude enough to set before your friends, what you cannot eat yourself.'

In the fourteenth century you needed nearly as many gadgets, and certainly more pots and pans, than you find in the modern kitchen. A contemporary list mentions pots, pans, cauldrons, pot-hangers, saucepans, wood and metal skewers, spits, meat hooks, larding-needles, pestles, mortars, sieves, strainers, colanders, large and small spoons, cheesegraters, etc. etc.

The fireplace where you cooked was so enormous you could walk in without stooping. At the back was a hook from which hung a cauldron big enough to hold two buckets of water. Grouped round were other big and little pots of different shapes, some hanging from hooks, some on trivets, in which food cooked.

At the front were the two great andirons, the uprights of which ended in baskets in which pots or jugs could be placed to keep hot or even to cook. On the front of each upright was a line of hooks on which rested the skimming ladles, scoops, tongs, pokers and forks, all with long handles because the heat of the fire could be so fierce that you could only work at a distance. Above all, the hooks acted as rests for the spits for roasting which were turned by boys, dogs in treadmills, or other mechanical means.

All the labours of the kitchen were organized and supervised by the cook who – and modern cooks will perhaps envy him this – had a large chair in which he could sit to rest and from which he could chastise inefficient turnspits or scullions with his spirtle.

Round the fireplace hung bellows, a salt-box with a lid that shut automatically as you withdrew your hand, frying-pans, gridirons, and waffle irons.

There would be casseroles on the floor, a long table against a wall, and on a shelf above it an assortment of utensils that did not need to be constantly at hand.

Elsewhere was a spice cupboard that was kept locked and a gutter-stone (a sort of sink at floor level), round which were bowls, basins, milk-pans, jugs, scoops and ladles.

Glasses were now becoming cheaper and no longer was it only the rich who were able to afford sufficient numbers for each diner to have his own glass which now remained on the table beside him.

Eggs have always been controversial. Erasmus said that it was impolite to use the nails of your fingers or thumb to peel an egg. The proper polite way was with a knife. In the 1640s a German called Harsdorfer, wrote that the Jews opened a boiled egg at the sharp end, the French at the blunt end and 'we Germans at the side'.

The Italians were reputed to not let anyone else use their personal knives. The Germans of the time saw to it that they had a knife each, but the French were quite happy if a whole tableful of guests had to share two or three knives. No Swiss, it was said, was ever without his knife which he used to help himself to everything but liquids, scarcely ever putting his hand into a dish.

Pork was the favourite meat. Pigs were useful scavengers and easy to feed. Being relatively small, if you killed one to eat, you were not left with quantities of meat liable to go bad before it could be used. Also it was easy to smoke and pickle.

A tenth-century dinner. Note the unusual round table and the way the meats are being served on skewers or spits.

Above: Medieval bakers at work.

Below: A fifteenth-century bakery.

The medieval table with its three tablecloths, one reaching to the floor at either end.

Then, as now, you washed your hands before sitting down to eat. Then, you had to wash again at the end of the meal.

Cheese and bread were two staple items in everyone's diet, high and low alike. Then fish, fresh from rivers, lakes or stewponds, or from the sea if you lived reasonably near the coast, or smoked or salted, but it was not until the fourteenth century that the Dutch discovered a way of salting herrings that made them keep for any length of time. You could also get stock fish, i.e., air- and sun-dried cod. Meat, as we know, was then eaten only once a week and on special occasions. It was either spit-roasted or boiled and stewed in small pieces until all the goodness was in the gravy; the resulting mush may have been visually unattractive but it must have been nourishing and tasty. People tend to think of medieval food as monotonous, but the recipes themselves prove that this cannot have been the case, especially after the returning Crusaders brought a taste for new, or rather forgotten spices and introduced the stay-at-homes to the use of rose-water and other scents for foods, to say nothing of colourings, especially saffron (yellow being the colour the Saracens considered lucky), and these must have revolutionized the flavouring and appearance of much of European food.

Many medieval towns had municipal ovens for use by those with no oven of their own. In country districts the manor had a bake-house that people could use for a fee. When houses came to be made of brick or stone, ovens were built in and private baking became general.

A private dinner – the same trestle-table, but here the two diners have a seat with a back to it. Note that men always ate with their heads covered.

Although the fork was used in the kitchen for carving, it was not used for eating at table until the seventeenth century, except in Italy. This drawing is after an eleventh-century miniature from a Monte Cassino MS. which must be one of the earliest pictures of a fork being used for eating.

Buying salt.

Buying raw sugar.

Li califes vint outre o toutes ses uertus
A ymon fist ceualier qui ert grans z corsus
T si bien se prouuoit z estoit si cremus
Qua senseigne porter fu sor tous esleus
z aymes lenkierka qui niert mie espdus
T ant itrencha de hyaumes tant ipcha descus

Cooks of the twelfth/thirteenth century at work.

Anglo-Saxons at dinner (tenth century).

When there were days in the week on which the Church did not allow people to eat meat, fish was one of the most important items of diet. For fresh fish, grilling has always been the best way, and the method illustrated here has probably been used for centuries. Put your fish in the wire holder, like a primitive Aga toaster, and lay them on glowing charcoal. Fifteen minutes later the tail and fins will be charred, perhaps burned off, and the fish done to perfection.

Once away from the sunshine of the Mediterranean, houses were cold and by our standards uncomfortable places. You ate in the hall or some other chamber that was not necessarily heated even in winter and undoubtedly 'draughty'. As a result men and women sat at table with their hats on and continued to do so for another 500 years. Apparently some parts of England were so short of firewood by the fifteenth century that it was being imported from Gascony and Languedoc, while in Northumberland and parts of Scotland they had taken to using coal.

Because people had only their spoons and fingers with which to convey food to their mouths, fish and meat had to be presented in pieces small enough to be eaten in the fingers of one hand, in other words without tearing at it. However neat and handy you were, you could not eat without dropping bits, if not on yourself, then inevitably on the table. As

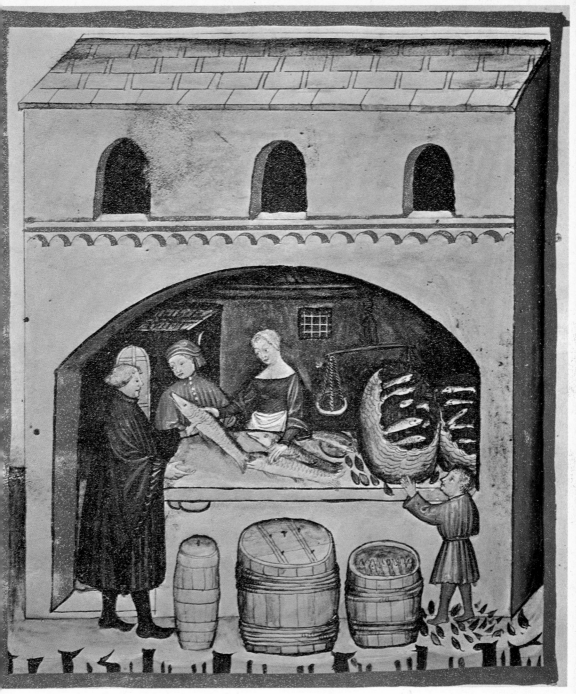

The fifteenth-century fishmonger sold both fresh and salted fish.

Opposite: The pork butcher's in the fifteenth century.

Outside of the kitchen of the Abbey of Fontevrault showing four of the five great bays, each of which housed a furnace-like hearth.

In the Early Middle Ages the arts, including those of cooking and dining, were preserved largely in the monasteries, whose kitchens had to cater both for the gourmand and the gourmet, and for the ascetic paying more attention to his prayers than to his pots, like that on the left. They thus ranged from the separate buildings of the great abbeys' vast kitchens, like those above, each with several great fires served by a complicated and efficient system of flues and chimneys that kept the air in the kitchen renewed, while the room temperature was such that the food kept warm, down to the simple open hearth.

A baker putting rolls in the oven and (*opposite*) the baker's shop.

66

Gathering saffron – a favourite colouring for food. In the Middle East yellow is the colour of good fortune and the Crusaders may thus have acquired the habit of colouring food in this way.

a result the cloth often needed changing after the soup, eggs and fish had been eaten. That done, the roasts and dessert were served. If the diners were to sit at table, the cloth was now changed again; if not, the company moved to another room where they had liqueurs, preserves, sweetmeats, ginger and other spices which they handed round among themselves without servants being present. This was when the spoon, a minor work of art made of precious metals, was used, rather than at the dining-table.

Since Roman times, goose eggs were those most used in the ordinary household.

It was not until people began taking their own spoons with them when they went out to dine, that they took to supping soup instead of drinking it, and so used their spoons at table.

As food had to be cut small and meats made to go round, carving was an art as important to the people of the Middle Ages as it had been to the Romans. In the days of the tourney, one of the rewards of victory in addition to the favours of your chosen lady, was often an invitation to

69

Several ladies at table.

A married couple at their dinner table about to be served a dish of eyes.

A late medieval painting of Charles Martel at dinner.

carve at the ensuing banquet. All in all, the post of carver was one of considerable responsibility. You were expected to get a certain number of helpings off each quarter of meat or each fish, and in the bigger households there would be clerks to check this and see that you did so. For example, a quarter of mutton was supposed to yield three helpings and a salmon twelve. In noble households the post of carver was reserved for sons of the gentry and in royal households the carvers were all aristocrats, and so were the cooks. Even the carver did not necessarily use a fork, for the rules granted him the right to eat what was left in his hand, and he was expected

A richly laid table with a wealth of silver on the buffet.

Judging by the expressions on the faces of this butcher's three customers camel meat was highly prized in southern Europe.

to do so in order to show that the food was not poisoned. The carver remained a person of real importance until personal forks came into general use, after which what carving was necessary was performed by servants either in the kitchen or at a side table, but you still took hold of a leg of lamb, for example, in your left hand so as to turn it this way and that as required.

In the thirteenth and fourteenth centuries the nobility breakfasted between 6 and 9 am, dined at 1 pm and had supper between 7 and 8 pm; but ordinary people started work at dawn, breakfasted with their

Charlemagne waits to dine until his food-taster (carrying the nef slung over his shoulder) has done his work.

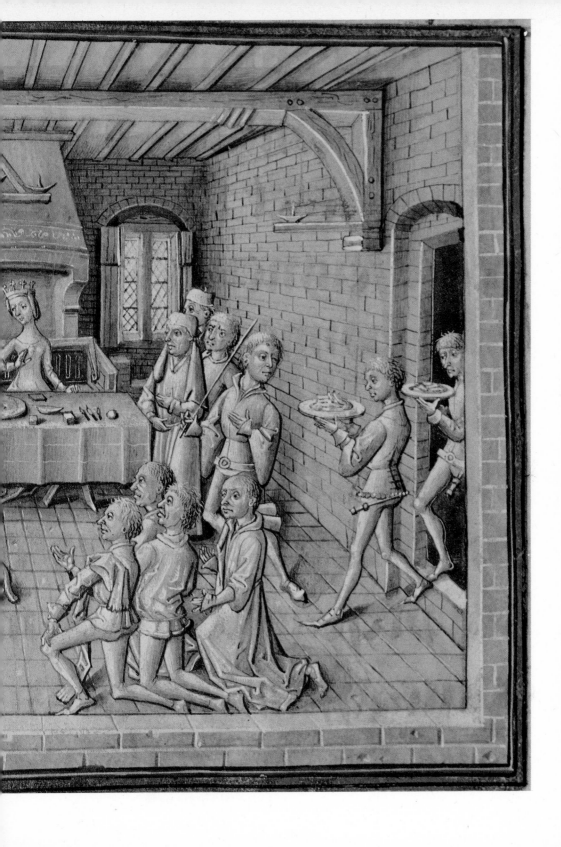

Detail from a still-life by Antonio Vassallo showing how beautifully pastry was made, and painted in the seventeenth century.

employers about 6 am and had dinner probably about noon. They left work at 6 pm in winter and 9 pm in summer and so could not have got home for supper before 6.30 or 9.30 according to the time of year. This meant that in winter they, and probably their employers, who stayed at work as long as anyone was there, so as to keep an eye on them, probably ate at the same times. In winter the curfew was sounded at 7 pm and in summer 8; but by the fourteenth century fires were covered only in religious establishments, so people returning home after the curfew hour could still get a hot meal.

Kitchen scene in a German peasant's hut.

In France in 1384, the *tondeurs de drap* arrived at work at sunrise, breakfasted at their place of work at 9 am, had dinner at 1 pm and left work at sunset, having had half an hour off for refreshment between dinner and the time of leaving.

On arrival at an early medieval house people washed their hands and dried them on a towel hung on the wall. Later it became customary for a servant to bring a basin and an ewer of warm water. The ewer was kept on its own 'ewery board'. The water in which people washed was specially prepared. You boiled up some sage, poured off the water, let it cool until

Hans Rudolph Daesch and his family at dinner (1537)

Some of the
cook's utensils in
a fifteenth-
century kitchen.

tepid, then added camomile or marjoram or rosemary and boiled this
with orange peel, perhaps adding a bay leaf or two.

People sat on one side of the table only. The table, consisting of boards
placed on trestles, was set up for each meal and removed at the end. If the
master of the house, or a guest, was of very much higher rank than the
others, he would sit at a separate table; otherwise the master sat in the
middle of the row of diners.

It was normal to cover the table with first three, later a single cloth of
various sizes. There was something symbolic about the tablecloth and
indeed the greatest insult you could offer to anyone in the fourteenth
century was to slit the cloth up on the right and left of him, thus indicating
that he was barred from associating with the others as having lost honour.
In humbler households where a tablecloth was not normal, if the master of
the household had allowed someone considerably his inferior to dine with
him, he would underline the difference in their ranks by having a small
cloth set in front of his own place, leaving his guest without.

In the fifteenth century there was a fine snobbery in dressers. For
example a sovereign was allowed six shelves on his dresser, a princess
could have five, a duchess four, a countess three, and a knight banneret
only two. Demoiselles and women without title had to make do with a
dresser without a shelf at all, just a top. Those from count up could have a

Off the fifteenth-century kitchen: a store with churn, plates in a rack, jugs, brushes, grater, etc.

velvet-covered back against which to display their cups and even jewellery.

The napkin had not yet been rediscovered, but now a deep pleated or gathered cloth, was fixed to the edge of the dining-table and on this people wiped their greasy mouths and fingers, but not their knives. Gradually people stopped carrying their own knives and instead used those of their host, who could afford to have a number. The Italians, however, still disliked using someone else's knife.

At the end of the fifteenth century, when Louis XII married Henry VIII's young sister, she insisted that he dine at noon instead of the customary 8 in the morning and go to bed at midnight instead of 6 in the evening. Louis, besotted by his young bride and, 'oubliant son âge et sa goutte', did his utmost to grant her wishes which were to have a good time and lots of children, so that she could be sure of continuing to rule as queen mother. Louis only survived two months of this new way of life.

A sixteenth-century butcher's shop.

The domestic time-table had been changing over the years. A hundred years after Louis died the elderly husband's death, the royal physician to Henri III arranged the following time-table for him:

	May, June, July, August	September, October, March, April	January, February, November, December
Get up	5 am	6 am	7 am
Dine	9 am	10 am	11 am
Sup	5 pm	6 pm	7 pm
Go to bed	9 pm	10 pm	11 pm

> Lever à cinq, diner à neuf,
> Souper à cinq, coucher à neuf
> Fait vivre d'ans nonante-neuf

had been the accepted way of living, now the jingle had had to be changed:

> Lever à six, diner à dix,
> Souper à six, coucher à dix
> Fait vivre l'homme dix fois dix.

Apparently the extra hour in bed also gave you an extra year's life.

People were now getting up at 6 am and breaking their fast after morning Mass – that is to say about 7 – on bread and a drink of ale or sometimes wine. Normally people did not break fast in company, but in private. Dinner, the main meal of the day, was between 10 or 11 am and noon. In big households, that is to say those of people of importance, a horn signal was blown when it was time to return to the house and wash before dinner. It was the medieval equivalent of our fathers' or grandfathers' dressing-gong. In France the signal was called *corner l'eau*.

The second meal of the day was supper which was between 4 and 6 pm. On the table would be wooden, pewter or perhaps even silver salvers for the main dishes, but probably no individual plates. People ate off trenchers, which were large slabs of bread about four inches thick, the bread being at least four days old. Each diner cut one off the loaf placed beside him as and when required. On this trencher you piled meat, fish, vegetables – whatever you were eating and if at the end of the meal you were still hungry, you could eat your trencher or, if you had had enough, you put it in the alms dish in the middle of the table along with everyone else's left-overs – or gave it to the dogs. It was not till much later that wooden trenchers took the place of the slab of bread – they were first used to put the round of bread on.

No one had a cup beside him at his place, unless only a very few were dining. When you wished to drink, you signalled to the cupbearer, who took a cup from the cup-board, filled it with whatever was going, brought it to you, waited until you had drunk, then took the cup away, wiped or washed it, and replaced it on the cup-board. In England people drank home-made wine and wines, both red and white, imported from France, Greece and Germany.

Each course would consist of a number of dishes. Most of these were not

Still-life by
L'Empoli.

handed round, but placed on the table for people to help themselves. The number of dishes put on the table was roughly proportionate to the number of diners: for 6–8 persons there would be seven dishes to choose from, for 10–12 nine dishes, for 14–18 eleven dishes, and so on.

One imagines the table groaning beneath a wealth of delicious-looking pies and pasties. They did have various kinds of pastry but not all were eaten. One was baked hard and was impossible to eat. It merely acted as a rectangular container for various forms of stew. The English called such receptacles 'coffins'. The pastry that you ate was 'fayre paste'. There would not be enough of the choicer and more expensive dishes to go round, so these would be handed to the more important people present. The nobility usually took their own servants with them to other people's houses and were waited on by them, it being their particular duty to see that their masters got the dishes they liked.

People still ate crane, heron, curlew, seal and porpoise, among other things, but quail, teal, woodcock and snipe had not yet begun to figure on menus. Nor had trout, flounder or herring.

Having set up the trestles and boards, the table was covered with its three cloths one at either end and one in the middle, each so draped that it hung almost to the ground on the diners' side. Next the seats and dressers were set in place and then the diners, having washed their hands, appeared and took their seats. The master of the household and his guests having seated themselves, the lady of the house and her daughters took their places, then the rest of the family seated themselves in accordance with their rank. After that the salts were set on the table, then the knives, ladles and loaves, and only then was the food brought in. Diners were expected to converse and at least pretend to be gay. After the main dishes had been removed, minstrels appeared and after they had performed more wine was brought in and more food served and finally fruit was set on the table.

Dinner over, the tablecloths were removed, the tables washed and dismantled.

Later on, it became the custom to put the dishes on the table before people took their seats, but the dishes remained covered, as they were brought in, both to keep the food hot and to prevent anyone sprinkling poison in them.

However well herbalists knew their job, it can never have been easy to poison an individual by stealth, and it is difficult to understand the obsession of those in high places with poison. Perhaps the job was so sought after as a sinecure that tasters kept their master's fears alive with dire hints.

In a royal household, the prelude to eating was the unlocking of the nef by the serving gentleman, who then wiped plates, napkin, spoons, knife,

The prince dines. Before him on the table 'the ship' with its poison test, his knife, goblet, etc.

Waffles have been popular for much longer than the 400 years since this picture was painted.

toothpicks, etc., with a piece of bread, an act that later became just a symbolic dab. This bread the *chef de gobelet* had to eat so as to prove that it was not poisoned. All other dishes subsequently set on the table were similarly touched with two pieces of bread, one being eaten by the *écuyer-bouche*, the other by the *maître d'hotel*.

Soup was eaten from bowls, one bowl to every two persons, placed between them. They took it in turn either to drink from the bowl or to dunk a piece of bread in it. With the eleventh and twelfth centuries it became more and more customary for women to eat with the men at the main meal of the day. Perhaps the first step towards women's liberation!

Opposite: This picture of Ahasuerus at table shows the metal dishes that only the rich could afford. Note the silver on display on the buffet.

An Italian kitchen of the mid-sixteenth century.

Above: A fishmonger's of the seventeenth century – de Witte.

Below: Kitchen scene detail – Teniers.

Opposite: A poulterer's of the seventeenth century – Mieris.

Husband and wife would normally sit together, if only because they had to drink from the same soup bowl and dip their hands into the same platters. The presence of women may not have had an immediate effect, but their influence on manners was enormous.

You now found the men, particularly the young, being told not to scratch their heads or chests at table, else they would be thought to be lousy, nor must they scratch their backsides, fondle a dog or cat. They were not to wipe their hands on their clothes, nor wipe their noses on the hand with which they helped themselves from the dishes. These injunctions give a vivid picture of what manners must have been. Even the books of etiquette that appeared in the fifteenth century were still instructing their readers not to drink with their mouths full, not to eat food on both sides of the mouth at once, and above all, 'let thy nails be clean'. By 1545 the etiquette books were telling the young not to put their elbows on the table as the 'insolent rich' of the new banker/merchant class did, and warning them not to drink more than three times in a meal. Such a drink, of course, was not a sip from a glass, but a gobletful drunk while the cupbearer stood behind you waiting for you to empty it and to take it away and wash it ready for the next person. You were expected to scoop up crusts, cheese rind, apple peel, etc., and put it in a basket on the table and to dispose of bones by throwing them under the table, providing you could do so 'without hurting anyone'.

When entertaining, people obviously ate in their best or largest room but when eating alone or *en famille* they ate either in their bedrooms – in those days all bedrooms were really bedsitters – or in the kitchen. The Connétable de Montmorency (sixteenth/seventeenth century) maintained that you could not eat well if you had an income of more than £500 a year, as then you tried to put on airs and insisted on dining in your hall and accepted what your cook provided, instead of dining in your kitchen and telling your cook what you wanted. A hundred years later, when Louis XIV was on his own he ate in his bedroom.

One of the most obvious changes wrought by the presence of women, was that people now began helping themselves with thumb and three fingers instead of the whole hand. The real man of the world became horribly genteel and stuck out his little finger as he helped himself, and that remained *bon ton* in French and German society for the next 300 or 400 years and has not yet altogether disappeared from ours.

The napkin that the Romans had used now came back into fashion. When not in use, it was carried, not spread on one's lap, but over the left shoulder or on the left arm. Later, when people began wearing elaborate collars, the napkin was tucked under the chin to protect the collar.

People now dined at permanent tables covered with a table carpet with a cloth laid on top, as the Dutch do today.

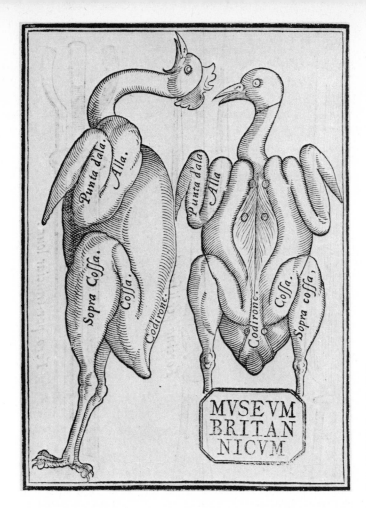

Carving was still all important and books were written on the art. This drawing from a book of 1581 illustrates the cuts for chickens and capons.

Dinner was between 11 am and noon, though the meal really began a good hour before, when carvers and those who were to officiate at the meal proper, had their own food. The time of the meal became later and later until people were dining in the early afternoon, and was followed by a supper at which perhaps more was drunk than eaten.

The French of the sixteenth century ate little bread and fruit, but lots of meat, especially pies and patties, or so the then Venetian Ambassador to France, Jirôme Lippomano, reported. As he travelled through France he observed how every town and even village had its *rôtisserie* and *pâtisserie* where you could buy all sorts of dishes ready cooked or oven ready. You could buy a roast capon, hare or partridge for less than you would pay for one in the market, all because those shops did such a good trade that they were able to buy in bulk. Obviously take-away foods were as popular then as now.

The really poor, Ambassador Lippomano reported, ate pork, while any

Above: Detail from Hogarth's *The Death of the Countess* showing the two-pronged fork (by the dog's paws).

Opposite: The sleepy servant – a Dutch kitchen scene of the late seventeenth century by Nicolas Maes.

Cardinals in Conclave dining. They were served from a special kitchen and waited upon with strict attention to protocol.

artisan or shopkeeper would eat mutton, venison or partridge on meat days and salmon, cod or salt herring on fish days.

There were two particular red-letter days in the gastronomic calendar, not 12 August or 25 December, but the days when the first herring and the first truffle were served. These were such great events that the cook appeared in person in the hall, torch in one hand, dish in the other, and served his lord with the first herring or truffle of the season. Normally dishes were served either by the panetier or the cupbearer, who had charge of the bread and wines respectively, hallowed by their association with the Last Supper.

Ruoia del Conclaue

Mazzieto

Riueditori

Tauola, doue li Scalchi
presentano le uiuande delli
R.mi, Alli reueditori.

Scala di ritorno

After the Fork

Three things revolutionized table manners and eating habits during the seventeenth century: the fork, the plate and the potato.

Some people, the Byzantians in particular, must have been eating with forks for a long time before this. A Monte Cassino MS. of the eleventh century shows two men at table using them, while, 100 years before that, Pietro Arseleolo, son of a doge of Venice, married a lady from Constantinople who scandalized the Venetians by insisting on eating her food with two-pronged golden forks instead of her fingers, so somewhere in that part of the world forks were known and used. They came into ordinary use in Italy and Spain in the sixteenth century and in Germany, France, England and Scandinavia 100 years later.

The French seem to have taken to the fork before the Germans or English. The German author of *Wunderliche & Wahrhaftigen Geschichten* (1648) makes one of his characters, who had been travelling in France, speak of the Frenchman's 'idiotic' habit of eating salad with a fork. 'How', the character asks, 'can salad taste decently if I don't eat it with my fingers?'

Using a fork meant tidier and cleaner eating. You could reduce larger pieces of meat into suitable mouthfuls without this having to be cut up for you in the kitchen, or your having to tear it apart with your fingers. You no longer needed to make little balls of your food to pop into your mouth, so it was no longer essential to have stews, ragouts and mushes. The use of forks also did away with the need for a clean napkin for every course as had become customary since about 1600.

'In the House of Martha and Mary' by Velasquez.

Swan pie served
at a musical
party of the
mid seventeenth
century.

The first mention of the modern plate in England was in 1641, when they
are referred to as 'white earthen trencher plates'. These were five inches
across and decorated on one side. You turned this decorated side face
down before you helped yourself. At first plates were used not for the main
meal, but afterwards in the chamber for eating fruit, creams and comfits
that were served when people had risen from the table and withdrawn to
what we would call the drawing-room. Soon, however, these plates were
being used for the main meal and there were also deeper plates for soup.

The transformation wrought by the fork and the plates together
inspired the following verses:

> Jadis le potage on mangeait
> Dans le plat sans ceremonie
> Et sa cuiller on essuyait
> Souvent sur la poule bouillie
> Dans la fricassée d'autrefois
> On saucait son pain et des doights
>
> Chacun mange présentement
> Son potage sur son assiette;
> Il faut se servir poliment
> Et de sa cuiller et de fourchette
> Et de temps en temps q'un valet
> Les aille laver au buffet.

Birds and smaller game were now served whole for guests to help themselves. The best pieces were held to be the wing of birds that scratched, the thigh of birds that flew and the white meat of the larger birds: goose, turkey, etc. The best part of a sucking-pig was the skin and the ears, and of hares and rabbits the saddle or the back. Porpoise, which counted as a fish, salmon or pike were cut in two, the half with the head being considered the choicer. The middle part of sole or weever-fish was best. Melon was served with meat, oranges with roasts. Truffles were still thought to be aphrodisiac and on the Continent eaten as a sort of dessert. Fruit was washed before you ate it. Cheese was cleaned – the Romans washed it – before being cut into small pieces which were offered, like fruit, on the point of a knife. Peeling pears, apples, oranges, etc., was an art about which books were written.

Carving, like all crafts or arts, had always had its own jargon. In 1813 cookery books were still writing of 'rearing' a goose, 'embracing' a mallard, 'unlacing' a cony, 'winging' a partridge, 'thighing' a woodcock and 'lifting' a swan. These were old terms, 500 years old at least, Wynkyn de Worde's *Book of Kerving* (1508) was using them and others such as 'breke' a deer, 'sauce' a capon, and 'spoyle' a hen. According to the jargon, you 'dispoiled' a peacock, but, tamely, you 'cut up' a turkey.

Among the upper classes, dining had always been a ceremonial affair, but as people became more cultured and sensitive inevitably some of them became irked by the presence of numbers of watchful, noticing servants; few however took the logical step of dining alone. One who did so was the

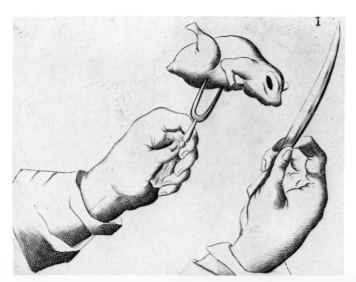

Carving remained an art which had to be learned. In princely and all great houses it was the preserve of gentry.

Marquis de Rouillac, who died in 1662. When his dinner was served, he entered the chamber in question, dismissed all the servants there and dined in peace and solitude. As he told his friends, he could see no reason for his servants to watch him chewing and he wished to be at liberty to fart if he so felt inclined. He had his pot on his table as well as his wine-glass, and a hand-bell which he rang if he wanted anything else. It is remarkable that a person with such sensible ideas should have been considered mad.

The author of *Culina Famulatrix Medicinae* quotes an anonymous medieval writer as saying 'woe to thee, O Country, when thy Princes eat in the morning'. Whether a hearty breakfast leads to bad government is debatable, but in England the habit of eating a good breakfast began to gain ground about the time that people there took to the fork. Now it was beef, mutton, salt fish, herring or sprats for breakfast which was eaten as late as 8 am.

In the middle-class houses you were waited on at table not by the dutiful daughter of the house, but by the son. The table itself was now

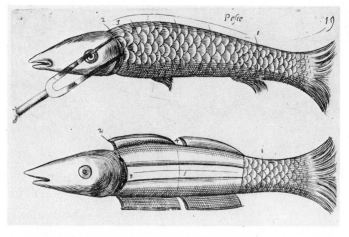

Some recommended ways of removing the skin from a fish and, *below*, of a pear

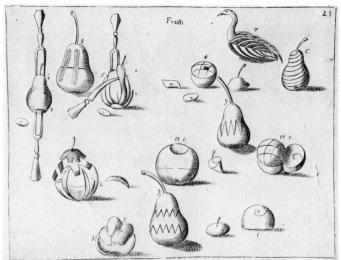

Above: One artist's impression of scouring a pan – and *opposite:* another's.

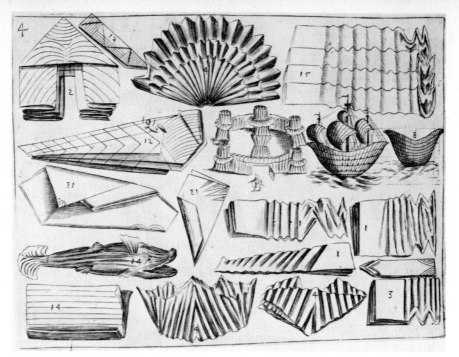

How the table was laid was of considerable importance and great artistry was employed in folding and arranging the napkins. Some were enormously complicated like the ship, castle and whale illustrated here.

often made oval or oblong, and people sat on individual chairs instead of benches.

By the end of the century it had become good manners to have a plate of soup to yourself. This was filled before you dipped your spoon into it. The books of etiquette now laid it down that you must convey food to your mouth on a fork (or in a spoon). Diners had a drinking-cup for their personal use, but neither these, nor the bottles to fill them were left on the table until the middle or end of the eighteenth century. Those who wished to drink had to signal to the servants in charge of the cups, who then filled their cup and brought it to them.

For banquets and special dinners you could have either 'service à la Russe' or 'service à la Française'. The former meant that hot dishes were not put on the table, but carved and got ready in the kitchen, then offered to guests at table. Guests of particular importance were always served first, but otherwise the guest who was served one course last, was served the next first. In the service à la Française all the dishes of the first course were placed on the table before the guests sat down, and subsequent courses all were brought in at the same time and similarly placed on the table, as a result certain dishes became cold and were not eaten at their best; but guests could carve for themselves the pieces they liked best and so on the whole, the gourmet preferred the service à la Française.

There were three courses: soup, fish and everything before the roasts; then the roasts and sweets; then ices, petit fours, fruit and cheese. The first course consisted of two *relévés* (dishes brought on to replace those first placed on the table, which were then removed), and four entrées; the second of two roasts and four *entremets*, and the third consisted of as many baskets and dishes as there had been main dishes and twice as many plates of dessert as there had been entrées.

With a dozen or more different dishes on the table, diners had to help each other and themselves to a much greater extent than we can envisage today, when we are pleasurably surprised if we are offered a choice. There must have been a considerable traffic of plates being passed along or given to a servant to be taken to the carver/server concerned for a slice of this or a spoonful of that. Such duties came easily enough when you knew what you were doing, but foreigners must sometimes have been bewildered, as was one Polish visitor to Britain, Lach Szyrma, especially when asked to provide the parson's nose.

The year 1680 saw the invention of the pressure-cooker. It was demonstrated in 1682 to the members of the Royal Society in London who were served a meal cooked in Denis Papin's machine. The food was praised, but the machine thought too dangerous for use in ordinary households. It did, however, demonstrate how bones can be made soft enough to be eaten with the flesh, and this is the method used in cooking salmon for tinning to this day.

The potato was introduced into Spain from America some time before 1570 and into other countries somewhat later. Nowhere did it gain quick popularity and governments went to considerable trouble to induce people to grow and eat it. In 1616 it was still a luxury in France and did not often appear except on the royal table. By 1750 the Scots had taken to the potato, although reluctantly, yet in 1764 the Prussian government was still making the cultivation of potatoes compulsory, but by 1800 it had established itself and become a staple ingredient of European diet.

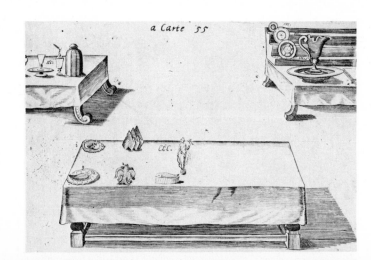

Places for one
and two diners.

Teniers's 'Woman Peeling Pears' – a country kitchen scene showing several of the cook's utensils.

This picture of Thomas Aquinas at table with St Louis shows the metal dishes and round platters used at the end of the seventeenth century.

Other familiar crops that were not indigenous to Europe were maize or Indian corn, rice and oil seeds. Rice which the Moslems had introduced into Spain in the eighth century was being grown as a crop in Italy in the sixteenth century and in southern France from about 1630. Asparagus, common in Roman times and then forgotten, was still rare and *pâté* of swallows a delicacy. Dates were regarded as medicinal (good for a child in the womb), and in May people ate garlic with butter, presumably like *radis au beurre*. Pastry made with beef marrow was the thing for apple tart and a classic dish was hoschepot or hot-pot, which consisted of beef, veal, mutton and lamb boiled up together with a host of pot-herbs and roots. This was not dissimilar to the classic Spanish *ola podrida*.

People only ate old birds where game was concerned, young game-flesh being considered indigestible. Turkey had been introduced from Mexico about 1520 and peacock, which the Romans had liked, was still a favourite because of the wonderful show it made on the table, but it was difficult to cook and tough to eat.

People ate much that we would not consider buying today: dolphin, heron, cormorant, crane, weever-fish. During this century (seventeenth) barley-bread more or less disappeared, its place being taken by rye or wheaten bread.

One oddity of the early eighteenth century was how, in France at least, it became non-U to masticate. The yokel and the urban proletariat champed and chawed, hence it was *infra dig.* for those who were anyone to imitate them by moving their jaws. During this mercifully short-lived craze one duchess had all her food reduced to a jelly so that it just slid down without chewing and almost without swallowing.

The author of *Les Dons de Comus*, one of the eighteenth-century classic cook-books, stresses the importance of the art of carving. According to him the Roman expert carvers had practised their craft to the sound and rhythm of music, and though not suggesting that one should continue to do so, he maintained that one must know how and what to carve. This was essential in a time when roasts and whole birds were placed on the table and diners helped themselves and any others who might wish a slice of what they had in front of them.

This same author was concerned as always with the health aspect: the merit of foodstuffs he, and those who thought like him maintained, lies in their digestibility and he laid down certain guide-lines: animals or vegetables that come to maturity quickly are more digestible than those that take longer; the smaller specimens are more digestible than the larger; those of dry fibrous substance are more digestible than those that are oily,

A peasant family at their meal. Seventeenth century. Adrian Broncwer.

Detail of seventeenth-century food from a painting by Caravaggio.

More utensils of the Italian chef of a princely household. Note the press and the huge fork used in carving.

fat or viscous. Those of a white substance are easier to digest than those of a darker colour. Things with a soft, agreeable taste are more digestible than those with a sharp, aromatic, piquant taste. Terrestrial creatures are more digestible than fish, and ruminants and vegetable-eating animals better in this respect than the carnivora. The meat of all poultry that is force-fed and animals that are kept indoors intensively, and vegetables that are forced or artificially grown, tend to go bad more quickly and thus are less suited for human consumption than those reared or grown naturally. Modern experience would seem to prove him right in this respect.

The famous eighteenth-century English cook-book by Mrs Glasse lists blackbirds, blackcaps, dotterel, fieldfares, godwits, knots, wheatears, gulls, larks, thrushes, ortolans and plovers among the birds one ate. Cod's head was accounted a delicacy as it is in Norway to this day. The feet and ear of pigs and calves were eaten and ox-palates and udders were still normal fare.

Manners were easier in the latter part of the eighteenth century. The mere fact of dining at the same table put all guests on a footing of relative equality, and the master of a household would have been ashamed to do anything to slight or condescend to one of his guests, however humble his condition. Fifty years later the picture was very different again.

The end of the eighteenth and early nineteenth centuries saw a revolution in the cooking process itself brought about by the invention first of the hob-grate (in 1746) and with it the spit-jack, the Dutch oven, the hanging

griller and the down-hearth toaster and then of the cooking-range which
Thomas Robinson registered in October 1780. Both were designed to
burn coal, which could not easily be kindled on a flat surface, but needed
to be raised on bars or other perforated surface. Robinson's range had a
cast-iron oven on one side of the fire-grate and a boiler on the other. The
oven was lined with bricks and mortar and had fillets for shelves to rest on.
It was very extravagant with fuel and made a lot of smoke. A considerable
improvement on it was the range patented by George Broley in February
1802 with its wholly closed top. This, the prototype of all ranges, owed
much to the impetus of Count Rumford, founder of the Royal Institution.

Born in Massachusetts Rumford became first a schoolmaster, then a
soldier, then a diplomat. A colonel in the British Army, he was knighted,
went to Bavaria to become General aide-de-camp of the Elector, then
Major-General of cavalry, Privy Councillor and head of the War Depart-
ment of Bavaria, finally being made a Count of the Holy Roman Empire
and member of the Order of the White Eagle. Retiring, he lived in London
where he founded the Royal Institution and later moved to Paris to
marry the widow of the famous chemist, Lavoisier. Rumford considered

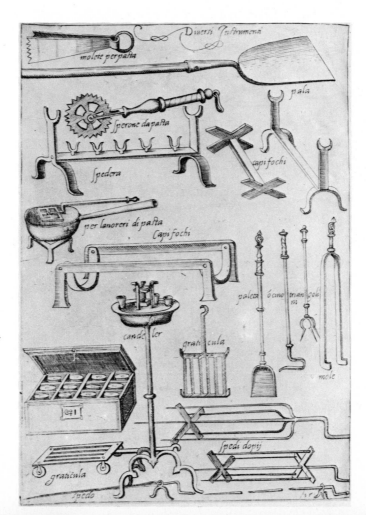

An Italian
chef's utensils for
making his
pasta, as well as
a spice-box,
grid-iron,
chandelier, etc.

Above: 'Bunch of Asparagus' by Edouard Manet (nineteenth century).

Opposite: 'Woman Peeling Parsnips' by Nicolas Maes.

his main claim to fame to lie in his work as a scientific and economic cook. He was an advocate of slow cooking and low temperatures and invented his own roaster. Meat roasted in this, he claimed – and many eminent persons who tried it agreed with him – tasted better, was more highly flavoured and much more juicy and delicate than meat roasted before an open fire. It was also economical: he used only 22 lb. of coal (worth 3d. at 25s. a ton, as it was then) in roasting 112 lb. of beef.

In Rumford's roaster the heat was made to circulate round a cylindrical oven, the temperature inside which was prevented from rising above 212 degrees by the presence of a tray of water. Thus the fat did not become overheated or burn. Two tubes that could be made red-hot allowed a forced draught of very hot air to brown the meat just before it was ready to be withdrawn.

Elaborately folded napkin for the King of Sweden's place (1961).

In one of the Count's experiments two legs of mutton (off the same carcass) were made exactly equal in weight and roasted, one before the fire in the way then normal and the other in the Rumford roaster. The two were weighed when cooked and that cooked in the roaster proved six per cent heavier, showing that it had retained that much more of its juices with consequent gain in flavour and tenderness. Both were found to be good, but the company showed a decided preference for the meat roasted in the roaster.

Rumford was shocked by the British households' extravagant consumption of coal in kitchen ranges and his work did much to improve the design in this respect.

The eighteenth century saw the revival of the intimate dinner and small supper for which the choice of guests was as important as that of the dishes, because now conversation ranked level with the food and guests were expected to contribute as much as the cook. This was really back to the Greek symposium and it brought with it a need for a separate room in which to dine, the *salle à manger* or dining-room, such as the Greeks and Romans had.

People and their cooks were paying more attention to quality and subtleties of flavour than to splendour and visible pomp of what was served. A new age of gastronomy had begun, in which the gourmet was as much of a personality as those of ancient Athens or Rome had been. It was a time when people themselves invented sauces and dishes, when more thought was given to food than perhaps ever before. Louis XVIII's cutlets were grilled between two other cutlets so that the one the King ate should retain all its juices and flavour and perhaps gain a little from the other two as well. At the age of eighty Talleyrand would spend an hour every morning discussing with his chef yesterday's dinner and the one to be provided that evening.

The cry now was 'good food before everything'. Food even became a literary subject (*Almanack de Gourmands*, the books of A. Beauvilliers, M. A. Carême, Dr Kitchiner, *Journal des Luxus*); of course people still entertained and ate in the old lavish way, especially in big houses. One Frenchman who visited England in 1802 and was invited to spend the day at Lord Lansdowne's described how he and the other guests assembled at 11 am for *déjeuner*, that is to say, tea, chocolate, eggs and rolls. They then went to the library for conversation. At 2 pm they transferred to the dining-room to partake of cold meats and Madeira, each helping himself to what he wanted. Dinner, the real purpose of the invitation was at 6 pm. Lord Lansdowne himself opened the door to the ladies who trooped from the library leaving the men temporarily alone, but following as soon as the ladies were in the dining-room. After dinner they all went back to the library where they were served coffee and, an hour later, tea, cakes, tarts, etc., thus making one uninterrupted meal of dinner and supper which was served at midnight and consisted of ham, Hamburg beef, pasties and cheeses. The whole visit lasted well over fourteen hours.

Compare this type of entertainment with the select parties being given a decade later by W. Kitchiner, the brilliant amateur cook whose work and writings (mainly his book *Cook's Oracle*) forstalled that of his now more famous contemporary Brillat-Savarin. Above the mantlepiece of Dr Kitchiner's drawing-room was a board on which was engraved: 'Come at seven – go at eleven.' At 9.30 those who were not able to face more food went home, while the others returned to the dining-room for a light meal with wine, ale, etc., and at 11 pm hats and sticks were *brought* in and the guests all obediently departed. On more special occasions, when the food was to be even more choice, the Doctor's front door was locked five minutes after the hour for which his guests had been invited and no one arriving after that was allowed in.

In manners the whole trend was away from formality towards not perhaps, the free and easy, but the cosy and more intimate. You dined among friends or with people who, if unknown, were of similar tastes and so at least potential friends. This trend is described by that self-appointed mentor on manners, the Rev. Trusler, who wrote at the end of the eighteenth century:

'Custom has lately introduced a new mode of seating. A gentleman and a lady sitting alternately round the table, and this, for the better convenience of the lady's being attended to, and served by the gentleman next to her.

Eighteenth-century kitchen by Antoine Raspal.

'The mistress of the house always sits at the upper end of her table, providing ladies are present, and her husband at the lower; but if the company consists of gentlemen only, the mistress seldom appears, in which case, the master takes the upper seat.

'Where there are not two courses, but one course and a remove, that is a dish to be brought up when the one is taken away, the mistress or person who presides, should acquaint her company with what is to come; or if the whole is put on the table at once, should tell her friends that "they see their dinner"; but, they should be told what wine or other liquors is on the sideboard.

'If any of the company seem backward in asking for wine, it is the part of the master to ask them to drink, or he will be thought to grudge his liquor.

'As it is unseemly in ladies to call for wine, the gentlemen present should ask them in turn, whether it is agreeable to drink a glass of wine. (Mrs. ——, will you do me the honour to drink a glass of wine with me?) and what kind of wine present they prefer, and call for two glasses of such wine, accordingly. Each then waits until the other is served, when they bow to each other and drink.'

The picture on the Continent, in France for example, was somewhat similar; the women all went into the dining-room ahead of the men, those nearest the door when dinner was announced starting the movement. In the dining-room, the host and hostess selected the four most distinguished ladies to sit beside them and the other guests just seated themselves as they chose.

Every writer on manners has discussed the problem of children's behaviour at table. Joseph Koenig, writing in Germany in 1832, had this to say: 'You have only to go once to the remoter parts of the world, or sit at the table of a father who, as so often happens, has allowed his children to grow up like little animals, to learn that clean, modest, quiet table manners are not innate or natural. It is largely a matter of teaching children early how to use fork, knife and spoon. Here, too, there are differences in ways and methods. The English, for example, lay the knife on the right and the fork on the left, and convey the pieces they have cut with the right hand to the mouth with the left hand. This method is a simplification and so it is to be recommended to people on the Continent, who mostly lay down the knife when they have cut with it, then take in the right hand the fork in order to convey the food to their mouths. In Bavaria, people usually lick clean the spoon used for the soup and lay it on the table beside them in order to have it for scooping up the gravy of the meat course. This, too, is the reason why the richer Dutch lay six or eight silver spoons beside each place. Food, of course, should never swim in gravy, as it so often does in the popular cooking of North Germany:

gravy properly thickened will remain conveniently on the morsel to be eaten and what is left at the end can be mopped up with bread.

'How easy it would be to guide the rising generation to adopt the English method and stop licking spoons, smacking their lips and similar habits.'

The nineteenth century was another time of considerable culinary change. In 1805 the first enamel saucepan makes its appearance and other minor technical innovations followed. In the 1840s J. von Liebig 'discovered' that if meat was put in to a pot of boiling water, allowed to boil for a few minutes and then set aside in a warm stove so that the water was kept at 70–74 degrees, the meat would cook to perfection. This is the principle of haybox cooking which was practised by the Jews in Juvenal's day (First century A.D.) and no doubt long before. The Jews used it to keep food cooked on a Friday so that it could be eaten hot on the Sabbath without reheating and so breaking the law. The Japanese have for centuries use the same principle for keeping cooked rice hot.

Country people have used small hayboxes to take their dinners out to the fields, when there was not time to return home and they wanted a hot meal. This is recorded as still being done in Baden in the 1850s. It must also have been in use in Norway, probably long before (how useful it would have been to the Vikings travelling in their open long ships), because at the World Exhibition in Paris a certain J. Sorensen of 27 rue d'Antin, Paris, exhibited a 'Cuisine automatique norvégienne'. The haybox does, of course, limit the cook's scope, but it is ideal whenever energy has to be conserved, or when you are using wood for fuel. The use of wood means frequent stoking, so that if you can leave your food to cook by itself, that is a great saving of time and fuel. The haybox is recommended for these

Table laid as in Queen Christina's time.

The still-life by Fyt depicts some of the foods of the seventeenth century.

reasons in Hanna Wisnes's *Textbook for Housekeeping*, the ninth edition of which was published in Christiana, as Oslo was then called, in 1872. Haybox cooking was a feature of the war effort in Britain during the World Wars. And who is to say that we have seen the last of it?

About the same time as Kitchiner and Brillat-Savarin were writing and discoursing on the finer points of gastronomy, a parallel movement in almost the opposite direction was gaining ground in Germany. The aims of the movement, which was headed by a scientist named Rumohr, was that we should all go back to eating plain simple food, that food should be allowed to 'taste of itself' and that it should be grown naturally, not forced, stuffed or interfered with in other ways.

Behind the basic idea, perhaps, lay a suspicion that the Irish author of *Domestic Medicine*, published in 1794, had been right when he wrote:

'The arts of cookery render many things unwholesome which are not so in their own nature. By jumbling together a number of different ingredients, in order to make a poignant sauce, or rich soup, the composition proves almost a poison. All high seasoning, pickles etc. are only incentives to luxury, and never fail to hurt the stomach. It were well for mankind if cookery as an art, were entirely prohibited. Plain roasting or broiling is all that the stomach requires. These alone are sufficient for people in health, and the sick have still less need of a cook.'

Partly of course, it was motivated by a growing boredom with elaborate, pretentious dishes, which was itself one of the reasons for the growth of nationalism in food which became more and more apparent at this time. This trend had been started, perhaps, by the difficulties placed in the way

Women buying spices at the apothecary's. This must have been a great convenience to those who cooked *à la* Borgia.

of travel and international intercourse by the Napoleonic Wars. Napoleon's 'tyranny' made lots of decent but perhaps not so intelligent people abhor what was French, and no doubt numbers of them refused to eat 'French food', as in the First World War certain people refused to listen to 'German music'.

The rights and wrongs of the science of dining seem to arouse passions as much as politics or bridge, and nothing is more controversial than the right way to dress a salad.

Alexandre Dumas devotes more than 1,000 words in his *Grand Dictionnaire de Cuisine* to demonstrating that salad is not natural food for man. Only ruminants, he writes, are equipped to deal with raw greenery in their stomachs, since raw plants are dissolved not by acids but by alkalis. It is, he says, an excess of civilization that has made us take to eating raw salads. The ultimate error is to make salad accompany a roast. To eat salad with haunch of venison, or with roast pheasant or woodcock is simply culinary heresy. One spoils the other. All game of *haut gout*, he considers, ought to be eaten by itself just with the sauce of its own juices. It is an act of great culinary impiety to allow your salad to be made by a servant. Salad is served at a moment when hunger is three-quarters assuaged and you need an aperitif to restore your appetite and thus it has to be perfect, prepared with loving skill and intelligence. Where, the inference is, will you find this except in the master or mistress of the house? And so the salad must be composed by one of them and at least an hour before it is due to be served. During that hour it should be turned three or four times.

Salad consists of vegetables to which certain aromatic herbs have been added, seasoned with salt, white pepper, oil, vinegar and sometimes with mustard and soya. Herbs, again, are of three kinds: pot-herbs, dressing-herbs and seasonings. There are six pot-herbs: sorrel, lettuce, white beet, mountain spinach (orach) spinach and purslane. Dressing-herbs are parsley, tarragon, chervil, chive, spring onion, savory, fennel, thyme, basil and tansy. There are twelve seasoning-herbs: garden cress, watercress, chervil, tarragon, burnet, samphire, hartshorn, lesser basil, purslane, balm and chives.

When seasoning chicory you put at the bottom of the salad bowl a stale crust of bread rubbed with garlic to absorb surplus vinegar.

Until recently salad-dressing seems to have been a peculiarly French accomplishment. After the Revolution several of the aristocratic refugees in England and America made fortunes as salad-dressers. In London, a young man called d'Aubignac accumulated £80,000 in quite a short period from the exercise of this skill, in which he seems to have used considerable imagination, as he is said to have used perfumed vinegars, oils tasting of fruit, soy, ketchup and even caviare among his ingredients.

Persian
cooks with
their mouths
hygienically
covered
preparing a feast
of many dishes.

Opposite: Young
man in a
Turkish inn
(seventeenth
century).

Dumas's own recipe for salad had six main ingredients: lettuce, slices of beetroot, chopped celery, slices of truffle, rampion and boiled potatoes. Salt and pepper do not dissolve in vinegar, as is commonly thought, and so it is wrong to start preparing a salad by watering it with a couple of tablespoons of salted, peppered vinegar. The correct method, according to Monsieur Chaptal, is to saturate the salad with oil, salt it and pepper it, before introducing vinegar.

The method chosen by the author of *The Three Musketeers* was to turn his lettuce from the bowl on to a plate, then into the bowl he put one hard-boiled egg yolk for every two people, mixed them with oil into a paste then added chervil, pounded tunny, pounded anchovies, mustard, one large tablespoon of soya, chopped gherkins and the chopped white of the eggs. All this was then thinned with the best vinegar he could find. He then returned the salad to the bowl and set a servant to turn it; as it was being turned Dumas would allow a pinch of paprika to fall on it 'from on high'.

The kitchen itself in which the utensils shown on page 113 were used. Note the contraption hanging from the wall-safe into which you could stick knives, spoons, etc. to tidy them away, and the running water laid on.

Opposite: Display of silver and sugar carving used on special occasions (seventeenth century).

Left: A Mughal meal served in the courtyard.

Below: Meal-time in a Persian camp.

Opposite: Hindus using plates made of leaves.

Islamic and Indian

Since the days of Darius what the peoples of Mesopotamia and surrounding lands have eaten and how they have cooked and eaten it seems to have changed scarcely at all. The Arab conquest of Persia in the ninth century imposed the dietary rules of Islam on wider territories, but otherwise little has changed except the importance attached to food at any particular time. For example in the thirteenth century Muhammad ibn al-Hasan ibn Muhammad ibn al-Karim al Katib el-Baghdadi, now famous in the western world as El-Baghdadi, whose cook-book was discovered in the Aya Sofya mosque in Istanbul only in this century was writing:

'Pleasures may be divided into six classes, to wit, food, drink, clothes, sex, scent and sound. Of these, the oldest and most consequential is food: for food is the body's stay, and the means of preserving life. No other pleasure can be enjoyed, unless a man has good health, to which food is ancillary. It is not prohibited to take delight in food, or to occupy oneself and specialize in it, for indeed God says: "Say, who hath made unlawful the adornment of God which He brought forth for His servants, and the

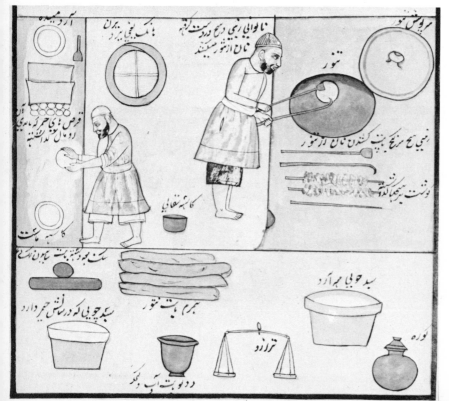

Indian (Kashmiri) cooks at work.

Bakery – from a Kashmiri sketch-book.

wholesome things of sustenance?" Likewise, whenever the Prophet was invited by any of his companions to partake of food with him which he had prepared to the best of his ability, according to his lights, he did not refuse. Lastly, a certain philosopher has said: "Four things comprise all excellence and perfect every blessing: strong faith, sincere endeavours, wholesome food, and healthy drink." It is proved, therefore, that there is no harm in taking pleasure in food, and specializing therein.'

Having established that point, which is also the assumption on which this book is based, the author goes on:

'Now men differ in their judgements concerning pleasures, some preferring food above all other pleasures, while others rank other pleasures more highly, such as clothes, drink, sex or sound. For my own part, however, I subscribe to the doctrine of the pre-excellence of the pleasure of eating above all other pleasures, and for that reason I have composed this book. . . .'

Four hundred years after this was written, the Chevalier Chardin described the Persians as not being at all concerned with food. They rose at dawn, that is at 5 or 6 am, and had a cup of coffee, some eating a little bread with it. Then between 10 and 11 am they had the first meal of the day consisting of fruit, cheese, milk and preserves. Their main meal was at 7 pm, at which meat was usually served. Even in the Shah's household meat was served only once a day to each person, though cooked morning

133

and night, because half the vast number of employees and guests had their main meal in the morning and half at the normal time in the evening.

When dinner was announced no one rose from where he was squatting on the floor: servants brought an ewer and the water in it was poured over their hands into a basin. Then trays were brought in and placed before each of them. It was only on special occasions that a cloth was spread on the ground before the guests, this was because more dishes and cups had to be set before each guest than there was room for on the tray. In polite society you ate with three fingers, unless you were dealing with couscous or something not very solid, when it was permissible to use five. Even if you had had enough, you must pretend to go on eating until the others had finished, because if one stopped the rest would feel they must do so too. Similarly you must not lick your fingers until the end of the meal, as that would indicate that you had finished, the others would then stop and the food be cleared away.

Food was mostly cooked in brass or iron dishes, sometimes also in those of earthenware. El Baghdadi preferred cooking-pots of stone, then of earthenware; as a last resort they could be of tinned copper, but there was nothing more abominable he said, than food cooked in a copper pot which had lost its tinning. Pots and pans must be left scrupulously clean: first scrubbed with brick dust, then with powdered potash and saffron

134

Above: Sixteenth-century Persians preparing a meal over an open fire.

Opposite: Persians at dinner, eating with their fingers.

Selling fish.
Note the large
scaling-knife.

Opposite: Making
chapatis

and finally with fresh leaves of the citron. None of your 'Hey presto and it's clean!' products for him, though he did live in the land of Aladdin. The rolling-pins of the East are wooden and the *batterie de cuisine* consisted of these, a long flat iron spoon and ladle, a ladle with holes in it, a vegetable cutter and scraper, a flat stone on which to grind curry, an iron or stone mortar and pestle, a few knives and little else.

Eastern hospitality was such that it could be an imposition. No one could ever be turned away, so that in catering you always had to leave a margin for the uninvited guest. According to the *Kitabi Kulsum Nanah*: 'should a thousand caravans of grief have deposited their burdens of affliction and distress in the closet of his mind, he [the host] must not show a single wrinkle of sorrow on his forehead, lest it disturb the serenity of his friends'. Also it was considered improper to ask a friend if he was hungry, because modesty would compel him to deny it.

The Persians and others of the East held that you must stop eating before the appetite was fully satisfied. Gluttony was considered peculiarly animal and held to be injurious to the intellect, the memory and the internal and external faculties. Also it destroyed the beauty and freshness of the features. Much eating engendered laziness and apathy in remembering God and became 'the parent of a numerous offspring of various complaints and diseases'.

Traditionally, you began a meal by eating a little salt, this being thought to increase the intellect and discernment. 'The composer of the mixed particles of the existence of men and genii, namely the beneficent Creator', says the *Kitabi Kulsum Nanah*, 'issued the following revelation to the melodious nightingale of piety, i.e. to Moses the son of Amram: "O Moses, order thy people to begin and to conclude their meals with salt, because to continue the use of this stomachic will wipe off the dust of the majority of complaints and maladies from the skirts of their existence; but if they neglect this injunction, the frigid breezes of many disorders will injure the flower-beds of their health."'

The fuel of the East is charcoal or wood or even dried dung. Muhammad El Baghdadi says that the wood must be dry and preferably olive or ilex, which do not give off acrid smoke. The wood of the fig tree is to be avoided, as should all sappy woods, as they emit too much smoke. But even in his day wood must have been becoming scarce, and by the twelfth century it was difficult to get and expensive.

When Johann Ludwig Küffstein was sent on an embassy to Constantinople in 1628, he painted the scene of a dinner with the Sultan that he had attended. The Sultan apparently dined in solitary state, in a small chamber with a window looking on to the hall in which his guests were dining: they sat at small round tables for four, five or six, and they sat on chairs, no doubt provided because being European, they could not sit Turkish fashion on the floor. Turkish cooking is distinguished by the importance it gives to vegetable dishes. Vegetables are not mere accessories to accompany meats and fish, but main dishes in their own right.

In Ispahan, however, as everywhere else in Persia, Chardin never saw a chair. You sat on rugs or carpets beneath which was a felt, and then the floor or ground. Against the wall were placed little hard cushions or

mattresses some three feet square covered with a fine cloth and you could lean back against these.

The Persians used to consider their fine complexions proof that theirs was the better way of living, pointing to the blotchy red skins of the Armenians and other Christians who ate beef and pig and drank wine. Not that the Persians did not drink wine. They did, as they had done in the days of their great poet Hafiz. Wine was still made in Persia as it had been for centuries, but the official drink and often the better, was sherbet flavoured with lemon, mulberry, cherry or pomegranate.

Two hundred years later when George Fowler spent his three years in Persia, he described the Persians as being fond of good eating. Their breakfasts, he said, were substantial, consisting of 'pillas, fruit, cotolethes, pickles, etc.' Beef, he said, they would not eat, not even the servants. The bread was flat and unleavened. They breakfasted at noon, after rising with the sun at 5 am or so, and dined at sunset, dinner being even more substantial than breakfast.

Above: Preparing a meal in a Hindu household. Note the leaf plates and how the cooks are women.

Opposite: Entertaining in the women's apartments of a Mughal prince.

A Kashmiri
butcher's shop.

Opposite: A man
selling kid in the
street, while his
wife tries to
swish the flies
away (India).

A traveller of the next generation describing an entertainment to
which he was invited, tells how, arriving about sundown the guests were
plied with water-pipes, wine and undiluted spirits, and how they smoked
and drank intermittently all evening. Dishes of pistachio nuts, etc., were
handed round, and spits of kebabs which he describes as meat enveloped
in a folded sheet of flat bread and threaded on a skewer. At intervals there
was music, dancers and other entertainment.

Supper was served about midnight, a cloth being spread on the floor
and on this were laid long flat cakes of pebble-bread (bread baked on
heated pebbles in an oven) which acted as plates as well as food. There
were bowls of sherbet with ladles for those who wished to drink. The
main dishes were pillaws, or chilaws, the only difference being that in the
pillaw the rice was already accompanied by the meat, etc., but in the
chilaw you took your rice and added to it what you liked the look of best.

He, too, remarked how rapid eating was and how little people talked.
Having finished, they all washed their hands, rinsed their mouths, rolled
down their sleeves, smoked a final pipe and went home.

The poor seldom cooked for themselves, but normally bought hot food
from public kitchens, each of which sold only one dish, its speciality.
These kitchens were really restaurants, for they provided carpeted
platforms on which purchasers squatted to eat what they had bought.
The fires in these kitchens were seldom made of wood, but of heath or ling.

Stews cooked in these public kitchens were kept hot by sticking wicks
into the greasy surface of the stew and lighting the wick. The flame drew
up and burned the grease and in doing so kept the food hot.

Sheep, goats, etc., were roasted whole, hung on a chain by the neck over an open fire made in a ditch, so that the heat reached every part of the carcass equally. Or they roasted small pieces of mutton or lamb, dipped in vinegar, salt and onion and spitted 'like swallows' – and this was considered the best way of all.

The Persian party was an all-day affair with guests arriving about nine in the morning. The time was spent smoking, discussing, sleeping after meals, praying, reading or listening to someone reading, or to lovely voices singing lays of ancient heroes. Serious people left it at that, but young bloods would send for dancers who performed in such a way as to excite their various passions and ended by representing the 'pleasures of love in a fashion that was altogether too free', with the result that these pleasures were then sampled (for the usual fee) as the dancers were all courtesans. Any in the course of their monthly off-duty period wore black taffeta trousers to advertise the fact.

The Persians used lots of ice even in those days. Sheets of ice were taken from lakes and ponds in winter, packed in salt, wrapped in strips of flannel and stored in pits which were then carefully covered. This ice was sold in the summer by the donkey-load.

At meals every person was given two or three 'leaves' of thin bread on which he placed a handful of herbs to serve as salad. You ate with your fingers, tearing the meat into small pieces, wrapping it in rice, adding a pinch of salt and swallowing it almost without chewing. People rarely spoke during meals which were soon over. The 'leaves' of bread also served as a napkin. At the end of the meal people wiped their fingers on this 'napkin' and then disposed of it by eating it.

The petlah bread you still get in Greece and the Middle East is used in

the same way, only it provides a pouch into which the food bought at a stall is put for you to eat. There is thus no litter of paper bags or newspaper.

At meals a bowl of sherbet would be placed in front of the guests, beside it was a long-handled wooden spoon with which you served yourself.

The Persians never kept food in their houses. Each day they bought only what was needed for that day and made that amount of bread. No dish was ever prepared in advance. The lamb to be eaten at supper was killed in the morning, the chicken just before it was due to go into the pot. What was left over would be given to the poor, and when the household went to bed, the cupboard would be bare.

The meats most commonly eaten were lamb, kid, capon and chickens – and eggs. Pigeon, fish and venison were eaten, but really only by the great of the land. The poor of the countryside might eat beef and veal during the winter, but seldom. Pig was forbidden them by their religion as was hare and all other creatures forbidden under Jewish law. The Persian doctors of those days still believed that people acquired the

Above: Another woman cook. Note the neat lines of the wood-burning stove and all the utensils.

Opposite: Mughal woman killing a peacock for the table.

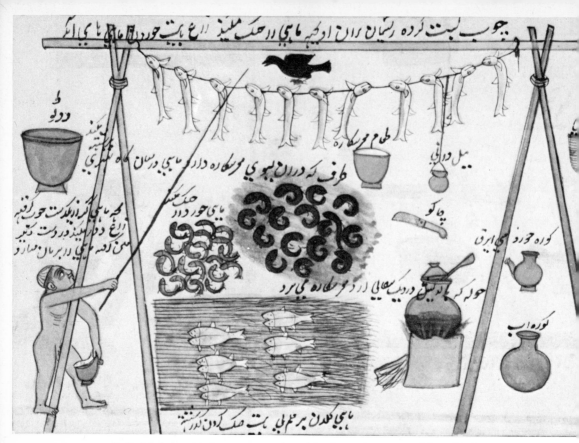

Split fish being dried and prepared, and having to be protected from birds.

characteristics of the animals they ate, and so lamb, innocent and without sin of any kind, was the favourite food!

All over the East what you eat has long been largely determined by your religion. Muhammedans have adopted dietary rules which are largely those of the Old Testament and probably once common to all ancient peoples of that part of the world. Prohibited was the flesh of hyenas, foxes, elephants, weasels, pelicans, kites, carrion crows, ravens, crocodiles, otters, asses, mules and wasps, but these are not restrictions that anyone would consider irksome. The old Institutes of Manu allowed the Hindu almost as much dietary freedom, banning little but mushrooms and vegetables raised on dung, blood and the flesh of birds and beasts of prey, but 'as flesh-meat cannot be procured without injury to animals, and the slaughter of animals obstructs the path to beatitude; from flesh-meat therefore let man abstain'.

Hindu worship of the gods was performed in the kitchen. The kitchen of the Brahmin house used to be a very sacred place, rather like a private chapel. It was divided by a low wall into two parts, the smaller for the fire

144

and the preparation of food and also acting as a pantry for the pickles and curry ingredients which all had to be kept safe from ceremonial contamination. The larger part which served as a dining-room, had an alcove in which the household gods were kept. These had to be honoured before each meal. When they had been given their due, that is to say been washed and offered food, etc., the doors were barred to prevent interruption and the intrusion of the impure, and the meal began. If for any reason you got up while eating, you could not sit down again and continue your meal, and if any impure thing (e.g. a dog) came in while the meal was in progress, or any lower-caste person approached, the whole meal would have to be abandoned.

In sitting, which the Hindu does on the ground on a low stool, the place of honour is at the right-hand end of the line: the others sit in order of age towards the left, the little boys and girls somewhat apart. Adult females do not eat with the males, though they serve them. The Hindu has his drinking-vessel on the left of his leaf plate and used his left hand for drinking. The higher classes used to have two meals a day: one at midday and an evening meal shortly before retiring. A good orthodox Hindu never took food or drink of any kind before the midday meal, but latterly a light breakfast of coffee and cakes has become customary.

When Fa Hsian visited India from China in the early fifth century A.D. he found that no respectable person ate meat, only those of low caste and, of course, the dancing-girls. These were allowed meat of any kind, except beef. They were also allowed spirits which was in accordance with the old medical texts that recommend alcohol in moderation. The number of laws governing slaughterhouses and the large number of those engaged

Fish being cleaned and scaled ready for the line.

145

A Persian feast. The cooks are wearing masks over their mouths while they prepare the mounds of food.

The early stages of preparation in a Persian courtyard.

in hunting and fishing show that many of the rules against meat were honoured as much in the breach as in the observance.

Rice was the staple in the Hindu diet. It was served with curds and cinnamon, cardamon and mace; or with ghee and mango juice, or with a sauce made of gram. Rice flour was used to make chapatis. Barley, wheat and beans were boiled or fried. Soup was made with stock of boiled vegetables. Although the Muhammedan will hang garlic at his front door to ward off the evil eye, or round the neck of his children to act as a disinfectant in an epidemic, garlic and onion were forbidden to the Hindu and any who wished to eat them had to go outside the town to do so.

The nobility enjoyed desserts of scented curds, creamy cheeses, balls of rice or wheat coated with sugar, thin slices of coconut and various spices either steamed or fried in butter. Fruit, of course, was eaten a lot, and so were curds, whey and salted rice, milk flavoured with spices and camphor, and milk cooked with ripe bananas were also popular.

The Indian fireplace was made of mud: the two sides were of equal length, the bottom convex in the centre so that the fire was raised, bringing the heat as near as possible to the bottom of the cooking-vessels.

Because of the Hindu caste system china and earthenware utensils and dishes could not be used, because, if contaminated, they could not be cleaned and had to be broken. Similarly spoons and forks, that others might have used were frowned upon. Food was served in the fingers, unless scalding hot, when it was permissible to use a wooden spoon.

However many servants there were in the household a Brahmin would only eat food personally prepared by his wife. If away from home, he either cooked for himself or his food was prepared by someone of the same caste as he. He ate alone, served by his wife, who first brought him water in which to wash his hands though he used only the right hand for eating. (The left hand, being used for the more intimate bodily functions, was not used in eating.) The food was served on a large banana leaf placed before the husband and when he had finished he rinsed his mouth without swallowing the water.

No man of good caste could take a meal in the company of foreigners or of those of inferior caste. Indeed there could not have been much jollity about eating at any time, because it was considered rude to speak to anyone during a meal, however many guests there were, and even to look at someone as he ate was the height of bad manners. The Hindu thus ate in silence, conversation only beginning at the end of the meal, after hands had been washed and mouths rinsed.

The Hindu had a horror of spittle – even of his own. He did not put his cup or glass to his lips so as not to contaminate it, but poured his drink into his mouth from a distance, somewhat as the Spaniards do when using a *porrón*. When eating between meals a Hindu breaks pieces off the fruit, or whatever he is eating and throws, rather than puts them into his mouth. Great care used to be taken that no particle of one's food fell on to one's neighbour's banana leaf, as that food would then be contaminated and the person concerned would have either to stop eating or get a new supply. Left-over food could not be given to those of lower caste than the people for whom it was cooked, unless they were casteless, i.e. the pariahs. Normally it was thrown to the dogs and birds.

Fermented drinks were forbidden to the orthodox Brahmin but popular with the Hindu. Only the ancient kings could afford wine made from grapes; others made do with spirits distilled from rice and barley, with the fermented sap of the palmyra and a delightful liqueur of raw sugar, pepper and distilled tomato juice. And very well they did too, by all accounts.

In the thirteenth century Indian women were expected to eat in their apartments before a banquet to take the edge off their appetites, so that they would not mind allowing their (male) partners to have the best pieces and would not otherwise eat or drink greedily.

Q. Craufurd writing of the Hindus at the end of the last century pointed out how much skill is required to achieve variety and tempt the appetite with the limited resources of the Hindu larder. He concluded that, allowing for differences in taste, Hindu culinary science (*supasastra*, which even kings were taught and in which every schoolboy is sufficiently versed to prepare his own dinner, if nothing more) leave the crude methods of Europe far behind. The possibilities of rice, he wrote, 'have never been suspected in this country.

'The Bengali's menu is varied, and his appetite enormous. Measure for measure your Indian will far outstrip the European in eating capacity.

A kashmiri cook fanning his fire surrounded by baskets of his main ingredients.

On the floor, four or five large dishes and as many small ones figure, consisting of soup, fish, curry, rice, cakes, puddings, porridges, pulses and fruit, but very different in their component parts from what we are accustomed to under the same names, and in their order of serving.'

In some castes a man has to bathe before eating; often he has to eat naked except for a loin-cloth. And in all households three meals have to be served: one for the men, a second for the children and a third for the women themselves.

Opposite: 'Not wisely but too well.'

Below: The Great Khan of China entertaining Marco Polo.

Chinese and Japanese

The ancient Chinese were convinced that vegetables, roots and cereals were the proper food of man. They liked meat, but they were not great meat-eaters. It was, their doctors told them, the worst possible food for children, and not really required by anyone until the age of sixty. Meat, in fact, was party fare which you ate on special occasions like the festival at the end of the old year and the start of the new, at the festivals of the fifth and eighth moon, and particularly when celebrating reaching the age of seventy, eighty, etc., and at weddings. On these occasions even the simplest homes gave meat to the aged poor and one of the Chinese expressions for great poverty was 'not even able to give a little meat to their old people'.

According to the Imperial regulations of the seventeenth and eighteenth centuries only artists could have meat every day. The most skilful of these, indeed, might have several meat dishes at every meal, but they were the privileged. In general, meat was eaten on two days a month at least, but only at one meal on each of these days.

You must hand it to the ancient Chinese! Instead of taking two, three or four prongs and fixing them rigidly in a handle with consequent limitations on their scope, they took just two, elongated them and while one was held more or less rigid, the other was able to move relatively freely allowing the wielder to pick up anything between a tennis ball and a grain of rice in size and to shovel, scoop, pin down, etc., quite as well as the fork or trident. This device they called *k'vai esz*, which the Western world knows as chopsticks.

The Chinese have used chopsticks for eating and in the kitchen since 500 B.C. or before. It is a clean, tidy way of eating, well suited to such fastidious people. You hold chopsticks in the right hand, taking them near the thicker end. One lies between thumb and forefinger and rests on the first joint of the ring finger which is held slightly bent: this stick is held in place by pressure from the basal phalanx of the thumb and it scarcely moves except with the hand. The other stick is laid resting lightly behind the third joint of the forefinger and between the tip of that finger and the middle finger which are kept together; it is held down by slight pressure from the tip of the thumb.

The knack lies in keeping the pressure of the thumb-tip light enough to relax the pressure of the rest of the thumb on the other stick which has to

A sixteenth-century traveller's idea of ancient Chinese hospitality.

be held more or less rigid. The thumb-tip is thus a fulcrum for moving
the second stick with the tips of the fore and middle fingers. The two ends
of the sticks must meet so that they can pick up a grain of rice if need be.

Chopsticks are between eight and ten inches long, made of some hard
wood, perhaps ebony, or ivory. Those used by children being shorter than
those used by women and these again shorter than those wielded by men.

Long, long ago, before the adoption of chopsticks, meat was sometimes
served in quite large pieces. After chopsticks it was cut small, usually in
thin strips. Most of China's land has to be tilled and as a result there has
never been much pasture, thus meat from the larger domestic animals was

Street butcher in China.

not often eaten – poultry, game and especially pork being the usual fare. The spread of Buddhism of course meant that fewer people ate meat, but those who did were still numerous enough for some sections of opinion to make propaganda against the practice. For example, as late as the middle of the nineteenth century, in one part of the country leaflets were distributed in which the spirit of a buffalo, pictured in the leaflet, related that hard-working animal's sorry tale, and added a warning to all meat-eaters. When this particular buffalo died, its flesh had been cooked and eaten, its hide made into drumheads and its bones manufactured into headgear for women. That this should have been done to it after a lifetime of drudgery in the service of man incensed the buffalo and its disgruntled spirit had complained to the rulers of the Chinese hell. It was told that those who killed and ate buffalo were well and truly punished for their

Selling vegetables in China.

sins, some being tossed into a tree of knives, others thrown upon a hill of swords. Others had molten brass poured down their throats or were bound to red-hot posts. Whatever their fate, none were born into the world again for ages and ages and when they were, it was as buffaloes. If you heeded this awful warning and refrained from eating meat, the pamphlet said, you could be assured of longevity and lots of dutiful sons.

The French missionaries, who studied the ancient writings, say that in cooking nothing seemed to have changed for thirty-five centuries, except for the invention of chopsticks.

In Peking in their day the people of high position and means ate the same meats as their counterparts in Europe, only not so often, that is to say; butcher's meat (including dog and donkey), game in season, venison and poultry. As far as the common people went it was not a question of

155

An early 'still' for 'brewing' Chinese wine, a necessary accompaniment to a good meal.

Two models of very early Chinese cooking stoves. Note the circular openings allowing some distribution of the cooking heat.

An ingenious fireguard protects this cook's face and body, but his hands must be tough to endure the heat.

what they ate, but what they did not eat, the former including things the good French monks did 'not deem desirable' and to which they attributed many of the fevers, skin diseases, ulcers, etc., from which such people suffered, food 'it is incredible anyone would think of eating and which we do not have the courage to mention', a phrase that certainly stimulates the imagination, if not the appetite.

In general, the French missionaries found that both in hot Canton and the Peking winter they were expected to eat little but vegetables, roots and 'herbages' accompanied by rice. This had always been so. Of meats, duck and goose were the favourites; pork that most often eaten. Butcher's meat was cheaper than in Paris and not much sought after.

The earliest surviving cook-book with measurements goes back to the tenth or eleventh century A.D. It was written by a Madame Wu of Kiangsu, but cooking was an art in China long before that.

Roasting a pig whole called for a special oven.

A Chinese steamer of 2000 B.C. The need for such a utensil shows how high the level of cooking must have been.

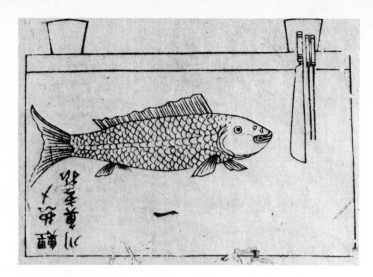

Ancient
Chinese way of
cutting up a fish.

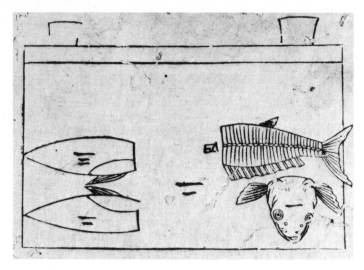

A study of the evolution of Chinese script written in the second century A.D. contains 9,000 characters dealing with food, cooking, etc. Included is mention of double-saucepans, parched rice, etc., but archaeologists have found double-saucepans dating to 2000–1500 B.C., so cooking methods must have been quite advanced then. Exactly how old Chinese gastronomy is, we do not know, but it is undoubtedly much older than that.

In 2000 B.C., they were using steamers (see page 159) and thirty-seven centuries later the French missionaries reported how the Chinese steamed their rice, bread rolls, fruit, etc. It was, they said, simple, easy and sure.

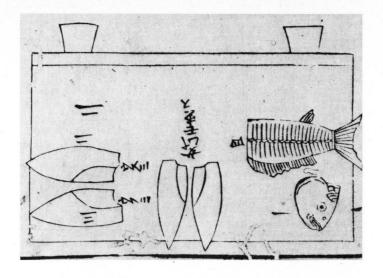

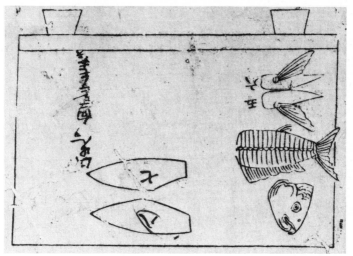

The Chinese it appears were 1,000 years or more ahead of us in making cooking-pots and pans of iron. These were numerous, made in many sizes and so cheap that everyone could afford them.

We think of rice as the staple of all Chinese cooking, but that is true only of that part of the vast territory south of the Yellow River where rice grows. Elsewhere rice was a luxury and wheat, maize, millet, sorghum the staple. Food found in a tomb excavated at Turfan included a roll of wheaten bread fried in oil and some *chiao-tzu* or what we call ravioli. This latter is further evidence to support those who claim that Marco Polo discovered *pasta* in China and introduced it into Italy on his return.

Selling poultry (China)

Even in the rice country south of the Yellow River, except among the poor, rice was not the main ingredient of a meal. Rather, it was a stomach settler and only appeared on the table after the main courses, i.e. not before the fried dishes had been disposed of. Soup, which would be served perhaps twice in a meal, was a gastronomic punctuation mark: a long pause which allowed diners a breather before they got down to serious eating again.

Early in the mid-seventeenth century, when Jan Nieuhoff accompanied the East India Company's embassy to China, he observed that among the better off rice was served at meals only on ordinary occasions, i.e. when not entertaining, and then only at the end of a meal. The Chinese dining-rooms he saw were not furnished with carpets in the Oriental way, but 'with pictures, flowers, dishes, and the like household stuff'. Each guest was seated at a simple four-square table well furnished with dishes. These entertainments, Nieuhoff remarked, could 'more truly be styled drinking meals, according to the earliest custom of the Greeks, than eating meals'. The Chinese wine 'brewed or boiled as our beer' and with distilled rice added 'had one good quality sufficient to encourage ebriety, that it does not make the head ache the next morning', was and is served hot or warm and sipped: 'They make several small draughts before they empty their cups, after the manner of drinking in Holland . . . they do but sip it off by degrees, never Potations, as we say Pottle deep.'

The Chinese, apparently attributed their long lives and excellent health, 'being very brisk and lively at seventy or eighty years of age' and their freedom 'from stone in the bladder' to their habit of heating everything they drank, even water.

The Chinese of those days ate very early. It was thought that if you did not eat until noon something awful would happen to you during the rest of the day. The informant of the French missionaries in China 100 years later said that on rising, even before he washed his face or rinsed his mouth, he took a spoonful of rice water and ate a small amount of rice. It was

– and fish.

北関夜市

明代汪劉鄭鮑諸家版畫（一五七三―一六四三）

一三五　海內奇觀插圖

Above: The pork butcher.

Opposite: Booths selling cooked food, Ming period. Note the Great Wall in the background and the constellations.

thought most important never to leave the house fasting, especially when there were infectious diseases about.

Little and often seems to have been the Chinese way. Some would eat five or six times a day, but the general rule seems to have been that in summer, from the fifth or sixth moon, when the days are longest, you had four meals a day: one on rising, which people did early, another at 11 am, another meal at sunset and a fourth meal, preferably light, two hours before sleep. During the rest of the year, three meals were held sufficient, but however often you ate you must always get up from table feeling that you could eat more. Repletion was frowned upon.

No dish brought to table was taken out again. Bowls and dishes were piled one on top of the other until by the end of the meal the table looked, as Jan Nieuhoff observed, like a castle. All left-overs were given to the servants.

You should, the Jesuits were told, be careful never to eat immediately after losing your temper. Rage causes the lymph secreted by the salivary glands to effervesce and with this leaven in it, it infects the chyle and has a distressing effect on the blood. You were recommended to start each meal with a little tea and end it with another cupful to rinse the mouth and teeth. This would help preserve your teeth into old age.

The feast or grand dinner-party was a late night and often an all-night affair. When given by mandarins there would be comedians to act and musicians to play while the guests were at dinner, 'to raise delight in their well pleased senses'.

China has been called, 'a sea that salts all the rivers that flow into it', and that, perhaps, is why the Tartars had so little lasting influence on Chinese gastronomy. Marco Polo has described how at his banquets the 'Great Khan' sat at the north end of the hall, facing south. He was seated

The travelling butcher.

Ready to entertain.

at a small table with his chief wife on his left, raised up so that all could see him and he see all. On his right at other small tables, but not raised so high, sat his sons and nephews and other kinsmen, their heads on a level with the Khan's feet. At other tables, lower still, sat the high officials and their wives; while the throng of lesser officials and officers sat on the floor.

Certain nobles had the duty of seeing that any foreigners present were instructed in protocol and the ways of the Court. The Khan himself was waited upon by high dignitaries who wore 'fine napkins of silk and gold' across their mouths and noses, like the Persian cooks in the picture on page 126, so that they should not inadvertently breathe on the Khan's food. The two eunuchs who stood ready behind his throne each wore a 'band of thick paper over his mouth and extending to the tips of his ears'.

All over the world the great ones of those days loved the ostentation of the buffet. The Great Khan's one was enormous, laden with golden and silver flagons and goblets of inestimable value. Even humbler members of Mongol society had buffets in their huts, on which were displayed skins of *kumiz* and other drinks and cups ready for use.

Two servants
waiting on a
high official.

Another similarity with the West is the standing accorded to the ruler's chief cook, whom the Book of Poetry twice lists among the most important officials of the State. And yet another is the fear of being poisoned held by the exalted. This led to chopsticks being tipped with silver, it being thought that any trace of poison would discolour the metal and so reveal its presence. For this reason a little silver disc was put in many cooking-pots to reveal by changing colour if any poison had been put in surreptitiously. What happened to those who had to produce an egg dish is not recorded!

According to Mei Yüan, the poet gourmet of ancient China, the accompaniments are to a dish what clothes and jewels are to a woman.

A restaurant.

There are, of course, some foods that should be on their own, such as eel, turtle, crab, beef and mutton and a fish called *hsi*.

Our eyes and nose, the poet said, are both the immediate neighbours of the mouth and its intermediaries: the colour and smell of a dish may be indifferent or enticing. Its colour should be as flawless as autumn clouds or as pretty as the marguerite, and the fragrance coming from it should fill the nose. You don't have to taste a dish to know if it is good.

Colour can be brought out by using sugar: but a good fragrance is not obtained by using perfumed spices or artificial sauces that alter the natural taste.

When a fish comes to table its flesh should be as white as jade and firm;

169

but if the flesh is the colour of powdered rice, it is not fresh.

The good cook begins by sharpening his knives, he frequently changes his dish-cloth, scrapes his chopping-board and keeps his hands well washed.

The poet gourmet said that there were certain things one must never do: add dripping to lard, let food wait or reheat it; to fail to use the whole (fish, turtle, duck, etc.) was impermissible as it was to press guests to eat or to allow flavour to escape by frequently lifting the saucepan lid to see how the dish was cooking.

The fat of fish, meat, chicken or duck should be kept in the flesh and not allowed to escape into the gravy, which would then have more taste than the meat. The fat can escape if (*a*) two fierce a heat is used, making cooking too quick and causing the water to evaporate so that the cook has to add more; and (*b*) letting the fire go out and having to relight it.

The ordinary Chinese reclined on mats, using low stools as arm-rests. Before the meal a jar of clean water would be brought to wash their hands. The used water was then poured into another receptacle. Everyone

Early Ming food-container.

Early Ming soup-bowl showing turtle and fish.

washed his hands before a meal. When liquor was drunk, the cup was washed if not each time it was used, at least very frequently. This would be done not by one of the servants, but by one of the diners wishing to honour the one who was going to drink, and he would wash his own hands before he washed the cup.

Like their European colleagues Chinese doctors in the old days had peculiar ideas about the medicinal properties of various foods. For example, they used to recommend a diet of rat's meat to halt incipient baldness. But, however strange some of their ideas, they recognized the benefits of frugality and one finds the Emperor Tai-Tsong (eighteenth century) telling the French missionaries at his court, who were very interested in Chinese food: 'The more I reduce the number of dishes coming to my table, the more I rid myself of my infirmities; the less I listen to my appetite at meals, the less I feel my age.'

The early Europeans in China listed the things the Chinese ate: wheat, rice dumplings, rice porridge, millet, boiled hempseed; celery, mustard,

The vegetable stall.

bamboo sprouts, ferns, duckweed, pondweed, taro hash, beans, pickled mallows, scallion, leeks, leek-flowers, rush roots and salted vegetables. The fish included sturgeon, bream, mudfish, turtle. Broth of beef, mutton or pork without or with vegetables; pork in gravy roasted with mustard sauce, sliced broiled mutton; dog, tripe and cheek, dried meats, hash of snail, elk meat or deer; pickled snail; pheasant, hare, quail and jay. Of fruit they ate wild grapes, peaches, plums, oranges, melons chestnuts and the Chinese date. Their vegetables included carrots, turnips, egg-plant, cabbage, spinach, peas, celery, onions and beans. The soya bean had been eaten in China since 2838 B.C. or before, so that it looks as though the French missionaries' estimate of nothing having changed for thirty-five centuries was a considerable underestimate.

Traditionally certain foods gain in goodness and healthiness by being eaten and even cooked in conjunction with other meats, herbs or cereals: for example, venison and hare need pork to go with them; gergelin goes well with dog; mutton with millet-chou, etc. Traditionally one of the choicest ways of cooking meat was in thin slices of certain kinds selected

Selling fish.

because they went thus together; the art of the Chinese chef lay in composing dishes in this way. There was little that you must not eat, but pig's brains and sheep's liver were among the few things that were banned.

It used to be thought that the fuel you used was an essential ingredient in the recipe: mulberry wood for boiling chicken, acacia wood for pork, pine wood for boiling water for tea, etc., even though coal had been used for domestic heating in northern China since time immemorial.

Hsien and *hsiang*, flavour and aroma, were the two essential factors in traditional Chinese gastronomy, and to these should be added, texture. The flavour of all food must be rich and robust, though never oily, or delicate and fresh without being slight. When flavour is *nung*, it means that the essences are concentrated and that the scum has been removed. To the Chinese way of thinking greasy food is anathema; you might as well dine on lard. When the true flavour of a dish is there, it is said to be *hsien*, but no margin of error is allowed. It is, of course, possible for food to taste of fat without being oily.

The third essential is texture: soft, tender, non-fibrous (*num*) or crisp

173

Cooking and eating in a Chinese household.

and crunchy (*tsuei*), and the contrast of textures is one of the great arts of classic Chinese cuisine.

Before the nineteenth century Chinese cuisine had been divided into four regional schools: Shantung, Honan, Szechuan and Hwai Yang. The gourmet recognized only ducks from Peking, hams from Yunnan, water melons from Hami in Sinkiang, etc. Later Cantonese and Fukienese were added to the list.

A Chinese plate in the Museum für Kunst und Gewerbe in Hamburg dated the late seventeenth century, shows a high official and his wife entertaining a guest. Each of the three sits at a small low table; the official and his wife next to each other and facing their guest. There are five bowls on each table and four servants are serving the food and waiting on them. By the nineteenth century, however, a round table able to accommodate twelve persons had become *de rigueur* for the formal dinner. The Chinese were still very particular about where they sat. The host sat with his back to the door, the guest of honour facing him and the guest second in importance would sit on the left of the guest of honour. Those seated near the host were either his most intimate friends or those of little significance.

As the guests took their seats, with a certain amount of polite reluctance, the host would fill up the little drinking-cups.

The table would already have been covered with a white cloth on which were laid chopsticks, spoons and tiny dishes, a bigger dish of almonds, another of melon-seeds, four dishes of fruits and another four of cold food: ham, salt eggs. The formal dinner would normally be a *chiu-hsi* or 'mat of wine' and would consist of thirty or forty courses, just like the European equivalents in the eighteenth century.

As soon as the guest of honour arrived, the host would order the servants to warm the wine, for the Chinese seldom drink cold wine or spirits. The dinner would normally start with two pots of hot wine being brought in.

Of the cold dishes, that of ham was the most important and was placed in front of the guest of honour: if there was no ham it would be replaced by sliced duck.

The host pronounced the magic word '*chin*' (please) and the guest of honour raised his chopsticks and helped himself to what had taken his eye. The other guests followed, the host waiting until the last.

175

Street booths selling cooked food.

When the four dishes had been sampled, a huge dish of shark's fin would be set on the table and the host would invite his guests to dry their cups: i.e. drain them. The host would then say '*chin*' again and they would fall to.

Then would follow ten 'fried dishes': shrimps, loin of pork, etc., that provided occasion for further drinking. Then hot orange soup and two kinds of pies. Then came ten 'big bowls': meat (pork) balls and fish balls.

Next appeared a large fish on a dish and duck in a bowl, and at this point the guest of honour would ask the host to allow the party to eat the rice, a tacit indication that the diners had all but shot their bolt. The host would ask his guests to 'dry their cups' again and with feigned reluctance would order the servants to bring in the rice; which they would do in four big bowls.

Obviously eleven or twelve persons could not eat all that food, so that

A Restaurant.

after the first few dishes, only some of the rest would be cooked at all, the others merely exhibited to demonstrate the lavish generosity of the host.

In the late nineteenth century the Chinese were said to pay more attention to the quality of their liquor than to their food. This is reflected in the wording of invitation cards which said that the wine cups had been polished to await your presence, though you might also be invited to come and 'eat rice'. The best of the Chinese wines was *shaoshing*, a yellow wine made in Shaoshingfu in Chekiang province, of which there were about fifty varieties.

Since time immemorial Chinese scholars have only had two pastimes: poetry and wine, and so the latter has a considerable literature.

Shark's fin, bird's nest, bear's paw – Chinese dishes may sound very different, but they are no more out of the way than cow's udders, pig's trotters, and other dishes that even the early editions of Mrs Beeton tells

The refectory in an ancient Chinese monastery.

one how to cook. The impartial gourmet will probably admit that there is more subtlety to Chinese cooking than perhaps to any other.

One of the difficulties that Chinese cooks had to contend with in the old days was the fact that not only did few of the guests arrive on time, but a self-important man would keep the party waiting two or even three hours on the grounds that he had too many engagements at that time. It was considered perfectly correct to accept several invitations for the same evening and attend them all.

In the old days men and women did not dine together unless closely related by blood or marriage. Even then an unmarried girl was not allowed to sit beside her brother-in-law. But in the cities this was all changed, when Western ideas found increasing acceptance in the first half of the twentieth century.

178

The Chinese used to have a god of the kitchen, who might be represented by a statuette or by just a piece of red paper on which was inscribed a sentence to the effect that the kitchen god ruled the lives of the various members of the family.

On the evening of every twenty-third day of the twelfth month a sacrifice of meats was made to the kitchen god. Rice was never included in the sacrifice, just meat and vegetables. After the sacrifice, the paper or the image was burned, the god thus ascending to heaven to report to the Pearly Emperor Supreme Ruler on the conduct of the family during the past year. A new god was then set up in the place of the old.

The staple ingredient of Japanese food is rice, its peculiarity raw fish. The Japanese way of cooking rice as described by Jukichi Inouye at the turn of this century, was that it was first washed until the water was clear, then it was put in a basket to strain overnight. The next day it was put in a deep iron pot, water added – it being important to achieve the correct amount – the pot covered with a thick wooden lid and set over a hearth. A small wood fire was lit under the pot and as soon as the rice began to swell, the fire was withdrawn and the rice allowed to cool gradually. It was then taken off the hearth and placed in a straw-holder (haybox principle). When it had stood long enough for the grains to be of the same temperature and consistency throughout, the rice was tipped into a round wooden tub. Properly boiled rice is soft, but each grain has a lustre and can be picked up singly with chopsticks.

After rice, the soya bean was at this time the biggest item. Soy sauce, made of the bean, wheat and salt, was used so extensively that salt itself was hardly ever needed. The bean was also the chief ingredient in *miso* (steamed and pounded soya bean with rice-yeast and salt) which was extensively used for soups. *Miso*-soup contains strips of radish, edible seaweed, bean-curd, egg-plant and other vegetables in season. Rice and *miso*-soup, plus tea, was all the Japanese took in the morning. Sometimes the family ate all together at a low table, but usually each person had a small tray about a foot square standing six inches or so high set before him. In the lefthand corner of the tray was a bowl of rice, on the right a bowl of *miso*-soup. In the middle was a tiny plate of pickled vegetables, also perhaps a minute helping of preserved plums, boiled kidney bean, boiled tiny fish or shrimps in soy sauce, or baked *miso*, that is shavings of dried bonito boiled in soy and mirin (a sweet spirit obtained from *sake*). It was unlucky to eat only one helping, so everyone had a second bowl (however little) of rice and soup, going to the kitchen for the soup that was left there to keep hot, while the rice was brought into the room in its wooden tub. Only the rice-bowl and the bowl with soup or other liquids that have to be drunk were put up to the mouth. Otherwise dishes remain on the

Preparing a meal in Japan.

tray and you transfer the food in your chopsticks.

When soups were not made with *miso*, they were flavoured with a liquid obtained by boiling shavings of sun-dried bonito, which the Romans would probably have recognized as their *garum*.

Pickled vegetables form part of every Japanese meal: garden radishes, small turnips and aubergines. These pickled vegetables have a smell that to the Western nose is horrid, as that of Western cheeses is to the Oriental nose.

Breakfast, they reckoned, was over in ten minutes or a quarter of an hour. The Japanese prided themselves on being speedy eaters and children were taught that quick eating was a virtue.

The Japanese midday meal was simple, too: vegetable soup, boiled vegetables (carrot, burdock, turnip, pumpkin) or fish, dried or cured (salmon, sardine, herring, mackerel) or perhaps fresh when it would be boiled or roasted. And, of course, there would be pickles.

The evening meal was the principal one of the day. It was little different except that it would probably include fish, boiled, roasted on an iron net and sprinkled with salt or separately coated with soy, or sliced

Serving a meal in ancient Japan.

and raw. The raw slices would be dipped in soy with grated radish and entrema (in taste a cross between ginger and mustard). Raw sea-bream was a great delicacy.

Though the Japanese did eat poultry, beef and pork, these made up but a very small proportion of their food, which was mostly fish and vegetables. These latter included potato, yam, taro, cucumber, onion, spinach and lettuce, kidney and horse-beans, mushrooms and other fungi, tiger-lily and lotus bulbs, bamboo-shoots, bracken and various seaweeds. Cherry-blossom and chrysanthemums were also eaten.

There are some 600 varieties of fish that the Japanese ate. The *tai*, a kind of sea-bream was held in the highest esteem and has had a book written about it. For eating raw, the next favourites were plaice, gilthead, tunny and bonito. Most other kinds of fish were boiled, but salmon was usually salted and herrings sun-dried. Sardine and pike were roasted. Eel was cooked in one way only: it was split from gill to tail, the backbone removed and the head cut off; it was then laid flat, bamboo skewers were passed through either side and it was roasted. While roasting, it was dipped every now and then in a gravy of mirin and soy.

181

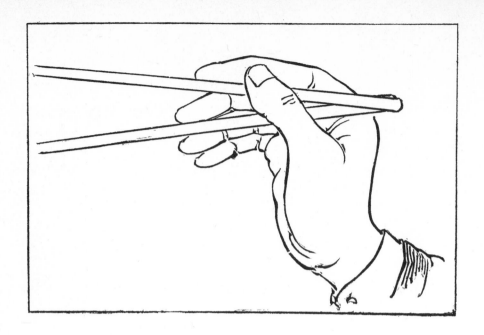

A Japanese meal-tray.

The Japanese eat all sorts of shellfish, mostly boiled. After boiling clams and sea-mussels and others with thin shells were served in a bowl of slightly flavoured hot water; while oysters were always shelled and eaten by themselves or with eggs. Crab, lobster, shrimp and prawn were other favourites and so were cuttle-fish and octopus. Cuttle-fish was often sun-dried. The hard flesh was sliced, then roasted and dipped in soy before being eaten.

The birds most highly thought of used to be the crane, Bewick's swan, the heron, wild goose and wild duck, the common duck, pheasant, quail, pigeon, woodcock and water-rail, as well as sparrow, lark and siskin. Most poultry was sliced and boiled in a shallow pan with onion and gravy of soy, mirin and sugar. The pan had a hollow in one side into which the juices could run so as not to saturate the meat.

Japanese meals never included dessert, so fruit was eaten at odd times, mostly oranges (mandarins) and apples, but also persimmon, which is peculiarly Japanese.

The second meal of the day was eaten at noon and the third at sundown. In summer the gap between the second and third meal was so large that a snack in between was often necessary, especially for those engaged in physical labour.

The Japanese word for cook means 'rice-boiler' and, particularly in the old days, when so much of the Japanese diet was raw food, this was indeed her main function.

North America

Anglo-Saxons are apt to forget how long the Spaniards had been on the American continent before the Pilgrim Fathers, disembarking from the *Mayflower* and no doubt feeling as adventurous as Shepard and Armstrong did when they stepped on to the moon, were greeted in English by an Indian who had learned his English in England. In fact the Spaniards had already been there long enough for the peaches, figs and other trees and plants they had brought with them, to have gone wild and spread hundreds of miles up the coasts and inland into the New World.

Soon others followed in the wake of the Pilgrim Fathers: from France, Germany, and Holland, and then from all over Europe, almost the whole world, they arrived in search of a new life, better opportunities, wealth, freedom to practise their own peculiar beliefs, or a refuge from political oppression. However little luggage they might have with them, they brought their eating habits and the need to have their food cooked as it had been in their childhood homes. By the time the various waves of immigration had swept the continent there were Albanians in New Hampshire; Poles in Buffalo; Ukrainians in New Britain; Finns in Delaware and North Dakota; Hungarians in Indiana; Basques in Nevada; Russians in Montana; Czechs in Ohio and Nebraska; Norwegians in Minnesota, Montana, Michigan, South Dakota; Swedes in Jamestown, Kansas, Minnesota, Nebraska, Michigan, etc.; Italians in New York, Missouri, Illinois; French in North Dakota, Wisconsin, New Orleans, along the Mississippi, Canada and New York, to say nothing of the Huguenots in South Carolina; there were Dutch on the Hudson, in Delaware, Iowa, Michigan; Germans in Pennsylvania, Oregon, Missouri, Cincinnati, Iowa, Wisconsin, Texas; there were Cubans, Croats, Welsh Baptists, Manxmen, Lithuanians, Syrians, Swiss, Slavs, Scots, Irish, Wends, Belgians and in New Mexico the descendants of the early Spanish settlers; and of course over on the west coast there were Chinese and Japanese.

Thus across the great North American continent you will find enclaves of European national cuisines enriched perhaps by new ideas and adapted maybe to new materials. Apart from those dishes based on maize and maple syrup, there are few dishes of solely North American origin, though the continent has contributed enormously to the world's fine foods and cooking. It has given us maize, potatoes, tomatoes, guava and maple

184

Maize was the staple food of the American Indian. Here Merian, illustrator of *Historia Americae*, depicts an Indian couple sitting beside a basket of maize with shellfish, octopus and another fish beside them.

American Indians roasting fish over an open fire.

Cooking down maple syrup, Indian way.

syrup, to say nothing of wild rice, which isn't rice at all, the Jerusalem artichoke, the blueberry, that bird with the 'great hanging chin', the turkey, and the okra you need for all true gumbo.

The new settlers found a profusion of game and fish in the rivers such as even their ancestors had scarcely enjoyed at home. Though in places they could scoop trout out of the brook with the frying-pan they were going to use, they had to learn from the Indians how to hunt and how to grow corn, tap maples, etc. Without the Indians' knowledge and expertise none would have survived.

Two hundred years later, the author of a book on Canada could still write this of the pioneer's life:

'. . . and by the rude road he has hewed out to his dwelling, spring up the red raspberry, black raspberry, the blackberry, often the strawberry. The wild gooseberry, both smooth and prickly, is seen on upturned roots, at the edge of the clearing. Wild currants, both black and red, are found in moist swampy spots, here are also to be found wild plums and choke-cherries (the last not very fit to eat); and a tangled growth of wild grapes . . . while high-bush cranberry shows its transparent clusters of scarlet berries. . . . On open lands . . . the ground is purple with huckleberry, the luscious bilberry; and strawberries of the most delicious flavour carpet the ground.'

Whatever man has done to Nature, Nature seems to have been remarkably good to man! Canada also offered the settlers' table spruce partridge and ruffed grouse, tasting more like pheasant than partridge. There was Canadian hare, rather like white rabbit, and those temporarily reduced to eating black squirrel complained that it was insipid, but the North American blackbird was a real treat:

'Most excellent pies may be made of the blackbirds of Canada, which come in great flocks upon the fields of ripe grain, in the summer, and commit great ravages on those farms in the vicinity of fresh lakes and rivers, where they assemble to breed and bring up their young. They are of a good size, fat, and tender and are delicious eating at the harvest season; and make a dainty dish, either roasted or baked in a pie. . . .'

Fifty years later, on the other side of the Atlantic Mrs Beeton was still

Making pemmican, a simple way of preserving meat.

Early kitchen in Hazard House.

recommending blackbird to her English readers, but her blackbird pie also included rump steak, veal forcemeat and hard-boiled eggs.

Although remote in distance, the early North American settlements were not in any way backward. For example the fork was introduced in 1633, when one was sent to Governor Winthrop only a few years after it first appeared in England, though the Spaniards in South America had been using forks for the best part of a century.

In the 1770s the Rev. Beecher wrote: 'We had wooden trenchers first, then pewter and finally earthenware. . . . Rye bread, fresh butter, buckwheat cakes and pies for breakfast. . . . We made a stock of pies at Thanksgiving, froze them for winter's use and they lasted till March.' This was nothing new to that continent. The Indians had for centuries frozen bread and other foods to make them keep in wintertime. (How many years ahead of the deep freeze?)

The fascinating thing about the story of North American cooking is how four distinct ways of life were being lived during the 200 years or so that it took to open up that vast continent to the white man. The same story in Europe is one of a gradual progression from open fire to open hearth, from open hearth to closed top stove or range. In North America, however, you got the unique picture of a whole people of pioneers clearing and breaking new land, building log cabins, living lives of almost medieval self-sufficiency; making, mending, tanning, weaving, rendering down passenger pigeons and other creatures to get oil for lamps and cooking, working so hard they had little or no time for refinements, though in many ways they lived well. Often they sold up after a while and moved on into other virgin territory to start all over again. Later another whole people of men were building railroads, felling trees, prospecting for precious metals, ranching cattle. They all lived rough in fairly primitive conditions. Yet all the while, in the settled parts, people in the towns and cities lived urban lives similar in their refinements of civilization to those of the merchants, bankers, shopkeepers in other cities elsewhere in the world, while in the countryside, people with plantations, estates and ranches were living the life of squires. And all this was going on not in different ages, but in the same age, at the same time.

In parts of the great continent cattle- and sheep-men would be eating

A spice-grinder.

Chuck-wagon.

from chuck-wagons like that pictured above, while at the same time in Newport, say, a Mrs Stuyvesant Fish could be dining 100 dog guests on fricassee of bones, liver and rice, followed by a dessert of shredded biscuit, a feast on which one dachshund at the original party ate himself unconscious and had to be carried out. Meanwhile on the other side of the continent a William Ralston could be regaling his guests with humming-birds stuffed with baked almonds and themselves placed inside a linnet, the linnet inside a snipe and the snipe in a goose, on top of which two canvas-back ducks were laid and topped with breast of goose. This remarkable dish had been soaked for six days in raisin wine, larded and smoked over sandalwood, before being spit-roasted.

The first cook-book to be printed in America was that of Amelia Simmons, published in 1796.

By the 1830s wood-burning iron cooking-stoves had mostly replaced the old open hearth. In 1807 anthracite was discovered and within twenty years the anthracite cooking-stove had become as popular as wood-burning ones. The ousting of the open hearth by the closed stove caused Catherine Beecher and her sister to write (1869):

'The introduction of cooking-stoves offers the careless domestics facilities for gradually drying-up meats, and despoiling them of all flavour and nutriment – facilities which appear to be very generally accepted. They have almost banished the genuine, old-fashioned roast meat from our tables, and left in its stead dried meats with their most precious and nutritive juices evaporated.'

For those without domestics the author of *The Canadian Settler's Guide* (1840–50s) took a different view of stoves:

'I would recommend a good cooking-stove in your kitchen: it is more convenient, and it is not so destructive to clothes as the great log fires. A stove large enough to cook food for a family of ten or twelve persons, will cost from 20 to 30 dollars. This will include every necessary utensil. Cheap stoves are often like other cheap articles, the dearest in the end: a good, weighty casting should be preferred to a thinner, lighter one; though the latter will look just as good as the former: they are apt to crack and the

Surveyor's cabin on the prairies.

Above: A kitchen in Pratt's Castle (1900).

Opposite: Preparing peaches.

inner plates wear out soon. . . . Canadian Hot-Air, Clinton Hot-Air require dry wood, and the common Premium Stove, which is a good useful stove, but seldom a good casting. . . . If you buy a small-sized stove, you will not be able to bake a good joint of meat or good sized loaves of bread in it.

'If you have a chimney, and prefer relying on cooking with the bake-kettle, I would recommend a roaster, or bachelor's oven. . . . An outside oven, built of stones, brick or clay, is put up at small cost. . . . The heating it once or twice a week, will save you much work, and you will enjoy bread much better and sweeter than any baked in a stove, oven or bake-kettle.'

The disappearance of the open hearth meant that frying-pans, etc., no longer needed extra long handles or feet to keep them off the ashes, so many designs changed.

The opening up of the vast new territories involved laying thousands of miles of railroad and felling mile upon mile of forest. The lumberjacks and railroadmen lived in camps, eating food cooked in quantity in a way not dissimilar to the huge households of the plantations before the abolition of slavery. Prospectors, cowpunchers and trappers often lived

Settler's cabin near Winnipeg (1880).

The day before Thanksgiving.

largely on their own, doing everything for themselves, leading a life that was essentially new to the European, but not to primitive man.

The kitchen was the focal point of the household and of many urban houses, though in the cities people with domestics tended to copy Europe and relegate the kitchen to the basement. The country kitchen had the family's gun hung up above the fireplace to prevent it rusting and often a horn to summon the men when dinner was nearly ready, hung beside it. Broken pewter utensils were melted down to make bullets. Little, if anything, was wasted. Even turkey or goose-wings were used as hearth-brushes for sweeping up the ashes. This 'canniness' the pioneer shared with the Chinese.

In the towns, domestics were mostly immigrant girls, many uneducated and not all that willing, their early day-dreams having been dashed by the realities of the New World, whereas those born to the country had so often been told that all were equal that 'service' had become a dirty word and 'helps' were hard to get and expensive. Not everyone could get or afford a servant, let alone several, as was the rule in Europe, and this stimulated the inventiveness of the quick-witted Americans who produced raisin-seeders, egg-beaters, syllabub churns, potato-peelers, apple-corers,

195

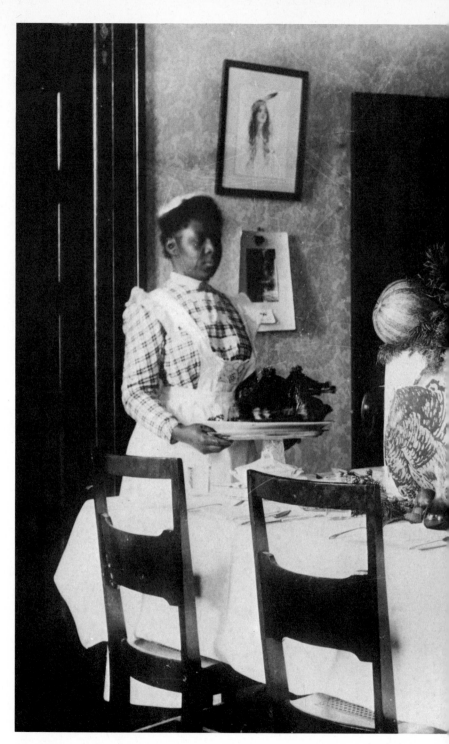

The traditional Thanksgiving Dinner.

Early kitchen range.

clothes-wringers, washing machines long before the need for them was
felt elsewhere. But the housewives of North America needed them – and
got them.

Except in the towns distances were vaster than anywhere in Europe,
except perhaps Russia, and so country housewives had to buy in bulk:
cones of sugar which required a special cutting implement and which
were themselves expensive; salt in great wet lumps that had to be dried,
barrels of molasses, vinegar, sacks of flour. You needed a large store to
house it all.

In Canada, as long as the ox remained the draught animal, beef was

Stove in an Oregon kitchen.

seldom eaten. At Christmas 'A glorious goose fattened on the rice bed in our lake, was killed for the occasion; turkeys were only to be met with on old cleared farms in those days [1837] and beef was rarely seen in the backwoods – excepting when some old ox that was considered as superannuated was slaughtered to save it from dying a natural death.'

North American inventiveness has contributed much to good cooking, not least what used to be called 'American cake'. This was a type of cake of a lightness hitherto unknown, due in part to the extra fineness of mechanically ground sugar and new techniques in milling flour, but most perhaps to the invention of baking-powder. An MS. cook-book written

in Toronto in the 1870s explains how snow makes a good substitute for eggs when making puddings or pancakes. Two large spoonfuls replace an egg, but the snow must be fresh-fallen, or taken from underneath the upper crust. 'It is the ammonia contained so largely in snow which imparts to it its rising power.'

Cooks used to add sal volatile to batter just before baking. Before that they used only eggs or home-made yeast and lots of elbow grease. By the 1830s purified potash obtained from wood ash, which was plentiful, or from burned corn cobs, was in daily use. This was called 'pearlash'. Then there was saleratus, a forerunner of baking soda and, finally, baking-powder itself, which revolutionized cake-making.

Emigrants took their manners and ways with them to the New World. Circumstances may have affected details, but by and large people went on behaving in the old ways, doing the same things, eating the same or similar things cooked in the ways of the old world.

Above: American couple in their dining-room.

Opposite: American husband and wife, Minnesota (1890).

Below: Christmas-time in Louisville (1900).

Lumber-camp kitchen, Minnesota (1900).

Mrs Frances Trollope, who lived in the United States in the early 1830s was surprised by the extraordinary amount of bacon consumed in American houses. 'Ham and beef steaks', she wrote, 'appear morning, noon and night.' Mrs Trollope was also surprised by the to her incongruous way eggs and oysters, ham and apple sauce, beefsteak and stewed peaches, salt fish and onion, etc., were eaten together. Bread she found excellent everywhere and common vegetables very fine, though she missed sea-kale and cauliflower, as she did turbot, salmon and fresh cod. She loved the rock and shad she was given and also the canvas-back (duck) which she pronounced superior to blackcock. She never saw a pheasant or a hare and laments the fact.

Dessert was placed on the table before the cloth was removed and consisted of pastries, fruit and cream.

She writes that mixed dinner-parties of ladies and gentlemen were very rare and 'unless several foreigners are present, but little conversation passes at table'. She disliked the habit she found of placing all the men at one end of the table, the women at the other.

Camping in Oregon in the 1890s.

Carving was an accomplishment every host and hostess had to learn. As *The Cook's Own Book*, published in Boston in 1845, said:

'Without a perfect knowledge of the art of carving, it is impossible to perform the honours of the table with propriety; and nothing can be more disagreeable to one of a sensitive disposition, than to behold a person, at the end of a well-furnished board, hacking the finest joints, and giving them the appearance of having been gnawed by a dog.'

The same author describes the etiquette of taking wine as practised in his part of the world.

'Soup being removed, the gentleman who supports the lady of the house on her right would request the honour of taking wine with her; this movement will be the signal for the rest. Should he neglect to do this, you must challenge some lady. Until the cloth be removed, you must not drink wine except with another. If you are asked to take wine, it is a breach of etiquette to refuse. In performing this ceremony (which is very agreeable if the wine is good) you catch the person's eye, and bow politely. It is not necessary to say anything.'

Above: Canadian Mountie kneading dough.

Opposite: Chafing-dish party (1895).

Early in the eighteenth century the 'well-furnished board' was indeed laden. It was set with soup, fish and the various game and creamed dishes of the first course all at the same time. (In Europe the soup might have constituted a separate, first course.) The dishes were arranged in a pleasing geometric pattern, what would otherwise have been ugly gaps being filled in with 'side-dishes' of pickles, etc. When each course had been dealt with, the dishes were all removed and replaced with an equal number of dishes of the next course: roasts, game pies, etc. Then would follow another course mainly of sweets.

Sometimes the tablecloths were replaced after each course. Often there were two, even three tablecloths one on top of the other, reminiscent of medieval usage, though now its purpose was to give an impression of opulence. Sometimes a scarlet cloth was laid under a fine damask one, adding a glow to its whiteness as well as helping to preserve the polish.

The finger-bowl had also crossed the Atlantic. *Complete Rules of Etiquette and the Usages of Society*, published in New York in 1860, says:

'Finger glasses when used, come on with the dessert, and are filled with warm water. Wet a corner of your napkin, and wipe your mouth, then rinse your fingers; but do not practise the filthy custom of gargling your mouth at table, albeit the usage prevails among a few, who think that because it is a foreign habit it cannot be disgusting.'

Minnesota kitchen (1900).

The art of napkin-folding that goes back hundreds of years flourished in North American society at the end of the last century.

Manners, published in Boston in 1868, lays down that:

'Silver dishes, where the means permit, should also be used: and also the finest kind of glass, cut, never blown or moulded.' Then came the North American's own contribution, the 'small can-shaped pitcher of engraved crystal, holding a quart' of ice-water, one of which was placed between each pair of guests.

Another thing the West seems to owe to America is the idea of the

206

dining-car on trains. The American Consul in Bradford writing about this country in the middle of the latter half of the nineteenth century wrote:

'The trains carry compartments fitted up with elaborate kitchens, having patent ranges and every utensil and appliance for cooking. Next the kitchen is a compartment arranged as a bar-room: there is a long counter before which are high stools, and where you may dine as well or as cheaply as at a Metropolitan Hotel. Behind the counter, against the side of the car, is a spacious sideboard, upon which you observe almost every variety of meat, hot and cold, pyramids of oysters, pates, pies and soups. I doubt if you would call in vain for any dish proper to America, and of edibles and potables peculiarly American – sweet potatoes, green corn, oyster roasts and stew, roast tomatoes, maize cakes, buckwheat, and the thousand species of drinks you find here the very best.

'Some of the railway companies have even improved upon this idea,

In a Minneapolis home of 1900.

Dining-car in the California Steam Express (1916).

carriages are converted into restaurants, with circular or square marble-topped tables placed here and there. You enter and sit down, one is handed an elaborate bill of fare, with the price affixed to the name of each dish, are served with neat appliance, and well cooked meat and vegetables, much as you would be in a city restaurant.'

It sounds as if the neat appliance most needed today is a time-machine to turn the clock back, perhaps especially as regards the life of 'the hurried driving American' living in a suburb: 'The merchant or lawyer who thus lives in the suburban town rises early, has breakfast at seven or half past, perhaps, either before or after the meal, does a little amateur gardening, props up the beans or peas, grafts or clips the orchard trees, cuts the grass, or weeds the flower pots, is off to the city by half past eight – At one he takes lunch at a restaurant or hotel; resumes business till four or five then takes the rail, the horse car, or the omnibus for home. A late dinner is already prepared for him and he sits down amid his family, thankful to return to the charm of a tranquil cosy home.'

Cook's Section

with 111 recipes from

Ancient Greece and Rome, the Middle Ages, the seventeenth,
eighteenth and nineteenth centuries, Persia, India and Ancient China,
and the early days of North America

FOREWORD

Despite the close links between Greek and Roman food, the two were very different in character: they employed many of the same ingredients but prepared them in quite dissimilar ways. The Greeks liked their food plain and simple and despised elaborate sauces and too many spices, though the fact that Athenaeus scorns their use shows that some people indulged in them; but the Romans, though many of their cooks, carvers and servants were Greek, delighted in food that combined many flavours. Roman food, as handed down to us in the rare descriptions and recipes that survive, had a highly original and very clear, refreshing and aromatic flavour. It is often sharp and piquant, never cloying or heavy, and puddings as such were almost unknown. One or two references to an egg custard and an earlier Greek cheese cake are nearly all that are given by the Roman Apicius and Greek Athenaeus. Figs, eaten on their own, or with bread, are often mentioned, and presumably fresh fruit was more to their taste than cooked desserts.

The Roman satirist Juvenal has several descriptions of food. In one he castigates the *nouveaux riches* for giving elaborate banquets for their friends, serving them with lobsters, asparagus and peacocks while their clients, writers and poor gentlemen like Juvenal are served with polluted Tiber eel and stale olive oil. In another he ridicules people like Apicius who paid a small fortune for one exceptionally large red mullet while people like himself are living in the attics of tenement blocks, unable to light a fire to cook a meal for fear of burning the whole building down. Juvenal's ideal is good wholesome country food, and in one of the later satires, when his fortunes have improved, he invites a friend to dinner at his home in Rome and tells him that he need expect no extravagant delicacies, but that he will be served with food from Juvenal's own farm: chicken, young lamb, new-laid eggs, fresh fruit and herbs picked on the hills by the shepherd's wife. As in all affluent societies there were eccentrics who craved the simple life in the midst of opulence. The German Rumohr in the nineteenth century and our modern health food movement are close parallels of Juvenal's disgust with over-elaborate urban living.

One of the fascinating aspects of these recipes is a chain that links much of the food throughout the ages. One can see links in Roman cooking with that of the Middle Ages through the use of such ingredients as saffron, cinnamon, ginger and almonds, oil and wine, as well as many herbs common to both. The early Persian and Indian food, which has remained virtually unchanged for centuries, contains these same flavourings which must be ancient indeed. Cloves, saffron, cinnamon and ginger occur throughout them all, and pepper, which is so accepted in our everyday food that we take it for granted as an essential seasoning. They reached Greece and Rome from the Middle East and lingered, in diminished use, in Europe until the revival of trade and the Crusaders brought them back to prominence. But the origin of such spices such as ginger and cinnamon is in the famous Spice Islands of the East Indies, and China and the Far East knew these exotic tastes long before the spice route had reached as far as Europe. Many of the ingredients freely used in classical and medieval times are considered extravagant today: saffron was widely grown and our previous olive oil was of so little account in ancient Greece, that when a cook wanted more heat quickly he would fling some olive oil on to the fire.

The instructions in the old books of cookery are delightfully vague, and very individual. The Roman terse and rather peremptory 'Pound pepper, rue, onion, savory, a little wine, garum, and oil'; 'Chop hard-boiled eggs, add pepper, cumin, parsley, honey – not too much, boiled leek, some myrtle berries'; 'Lay all in a dish, when it is set, sprinkle with pepper and serve.' The medieval cooks instruct one 'to take' this or that 'and seeth hem wel in gode broth, take wyne greke and do thereto with a porcion of vynegar' . . . 'seeth hem a litel on the fyr and when 'tis done serve it forth'. Sometimes one is even told to 'messe if forth'. We are so used to minute instructions for weights and measures, method and oven temperatures that at first it seems strange to 'strew on enow gode powdour' or to 'do it wel', but, after all, cooking has always been a matter of good judgement and individual taste. The cooks of the Middle Ages give us all the necessary ingredients, a guide to the method, and leave us with the inspiration to create a good dish. Occasionally their instructions are amazingly precise as with their famous recipe for 'Lamprays bake'. *Take and make fayre round cofyns[1] of fyne paste, and take fressche lampreys and late hem blode 3 fyngerys with-in the tayle, and lat them blode in a vesselle, and late hym deye in the same vesselle in the same blode; then take browne brede, and kyt it and stepe it in the vinegre, and drew thorw a straynoure; than take the same blode, and powder of canel (cinnamon) and cast ther-to tyl it be brown; then cast ther-to powder Peppir, Salt and Wyne a lytelle, that it be not to strong of vinegre. An skald the lampray, and pare hem clene, and couch hym round on the cofyn tyl he be helyd; then keyvere hym fayre with a lede, ave a lytel hole in the mydelle and at the hool, blow in the cofynne with thin mouthe a gode blast of wynde. And sodenly stoppe the hole, that the wynd a-byde with ynne, to reyse uppe the cofynne, that he fall nowt a-downne.* We have

[1] A paste shell of deep rectangular shape, often not eaten but used simply as a container.

baking powder and butter and eggs for their lightening effects on flour, so have not felt impelled towards this ingenious trick with a 'gode blaste of wynde'.

As in the earlier Roman dishes the medieval recipes also used lots of herbs and spices, as well as oil and wine. There are more sweets, but one gets the impression that fresh fruit was eaten whenever it was in season, and the recipes for puddings use dried fruits such as dates, figs and raisins, as well as apples and pears which store well, so presumably cooked desserts were mostly eaten in the winter and spring, although there is a recipe for cherries at the feast of St John the Baptist. Some of the recipes using dried fruit were laced with wine and ginger, cinnamon and cloves and provide a most delicious warm and spicy aroma on a wintry day. There were a great many appetizing ways of cooking meat, poultry and vegetables. The varieties of fish recommended are sometimes depressing as so many types are now scarce or nearly extinct. Porpoises were considered fish, and recipes for their preparation and cooking were given, also for many lake and river fish, such as roach, tench and perch, and the rare lamprey, which suggests that their environment was beautifully clear and unpolluted compared with that of today, as anyone who has tried the muddy flavour of roach or tench will know.

There has been a lot of historical nonsense talked about medieval food, most of it guesswork or based on a misunderstanding of the recipes, implying that what they ate was governed by such factors as decomposing meat which needed disguising with a mass of strong spices to make it edible, or the lack of forks, even lack of teeth! All these theories tend to ignore the natural incentive for all cooks to prepare food that tastes delicious and also looks appetizing. The people of the Middle Ages were concerned with the appearance of their food. They used 'saunders' made from sandalwood as a rich red colouring, and saffron is often mentioned purely as a colouring agent; dishes were 'endored', (gilded) or 'flourished', decorated with egg yolks or ground spices or even the vastly expensive sugar to add the final touches. Medieval food would not have been so misinterpreted if it had been cooked from the many delicious recipes available to us, and judged by the results.

By the seventeenth century the fork was firmly established and the medieval style of cooking had virtually disappeared. But the fork was not the only factor which changed the type of food eaten by the well-to-do in Western Europe: the increased availability and cheapness of sugar played its part as did the gradual introduction of new ingredients from the Americas and quicker communication with the Far East (Drake is reported to have been forced to jettison several tons of cloves when the *Golden Hind* ran aground). The people at this time seem to have used a wider variety of vegetables and many more members of the cabbage family, like cauliflower and broccoli, are mentioned. There also seems to be a change in the character of the recipes: gone are the long lists of spices and herbs and the multiplicity of ingredients, instead we find perhaps only two or three flavourings which will complement or contrast with each other. Cooks no longer wish to alter the original taste of the food but rather to enhance it with other tastes. It is impossible to be sure of the reason for this: food obviously reflects, to a certain extent, the character of the society which eats it, but it is perhaps too facile to say that the rich late medieval food reflected the love of extravagance, the sumptuousness of dress and the intricacy of architecture, while the seventeenth century's more subtle cooking reflected the return to classical simplicity of, for example, Palladian architecture and the classical forms of literature. Whatever the reason the new Italian style of cooking was spreading north and west and laying the foundations for the *haute cuisine* of the nineteenth century.

Eighteenth- and nineteenth-century Britain provided the golden age of cheap, efficient labour and lavish abundance in the kitchen. Huge amounts of butter, cream and eggs were used in almost all the recipes, and have had to be reduced in quantity for smaller modern families and more modest modern tastes. Legs of veal, pounds of lean ham and several chickens might be used simply for a stock with which to enrich a sauce. Almonds were freely used, as in all the European cooking from Roman times onwards, they were not expensive as they are today. One realizes from the recipes that nothing was too much trouble and the most gloriously rich ingredients were not considered extravagant. One sometimes finds patronizing references to French cooking, though whether dictated by politics or taste one does not know, and frequently patronizing comments on the simplicity and thick-headedness of servants in general. Many recipes have comments of a medical nature such as 'this dish cannot be said to contain either gout or scurvy' or 'this is a very wholesome soup for all ages and constitutions, and will be very proper for those who the day before have plentifully eat of a fiery turtle soup'. When simple soups could no longer assuage the pangs of indigestion, a trip to Bath or to Tunbridge Wells might be necessary. Here the sufferer would not only 'take the waters', and unaccustomed exercise, but would also be provided with plainer food. At Tunbridge Wells a delicious but wholesome speciality was wheatear pie. The birds were trapped on the South Downs and brought in quantities to the Wells every day where they were eagerly devoured by the ailing gourmands to the great detriment of the wheatears. The sweets, at this time, were perfumed with ambergris or strewn with sweetmeats. Some of them bear delightfully fulsome titles such as 'The best Orange pudding that ever was Tasted', 'To make Westphalia-Hams; absolutely the best way to do them', or 'this was given by one of the nicest

House-wives in England; and is as good as ever was made'. Such confidence, and such abundance!

There are recipes for heron, swan, curlew, lapwing and every sort of game; the countryside was still teeming with wild life. They tackled recipes for the captains of ships, 'to make a catchup that will keep twenty years. You may carry it to the Indies.' They loved to disguise dishes, and give ways of serving venison that is not venison: 'If you use mutton over 5 years old no one will discover the deception'; or to 'dress halibut in the manner of Scotch collops during Lent'. There are many recipes for the sick, and they were not even afraid to tackle cures for the most dangerous maladies. Along with the descriptions of delicious foods are remedies such as 'a certain cure for the bite of a mad dog'; 'receipt against the plague'; and a recipe for 'hysterical water' containing so many poisons such as 'mistletoe of the oak' that though sensibly diluted, the drink would have had a dramatically stupefying effect. There is advice on 'how to keep clear from buggs' and 'how to wash silver lace that has tarnished' as well as to 'prevent the infection among horned cattle'. Every household was self-sufficient and the housewife had to be cook, brewer, baker and pharmacist. The wonder is she had time left to dream up such delectable dishes.

However, the resourcefulness of the eighteenth- or nineteenth-century housewife was small compared with that of the early American settlers' wives. They not only had to be able to turn their hands to any and everything, but also had to be prepared to start with a life of camping, then adapt themselves to a settled farm and finally, if they were lucky, perhaps to become the grand lady of a large household. They had to cope with a bewildering array of new ingredients when they first arrived: one of the most important was Indian corn, or maize, and another the green, red and yellow peppers and chillies of the Mexican Indians which so influenced the cooking in the south-western United States. The Creole and French influence on Southern cooking is very noticeable and has provided a most happy blend of traditions. Pennsylvania produced a special type of German cooking brought by the early settlers who came to be known as the Pennsylvania 'Dutch', a corruption of the word *Deutsch*. They were rightly famous for their home-baking, and wholesome and nourishing dishes. There is an appetizing homespun quality about most of the early American recipes, New England and the South providing the more sophisticated cooking, but as well as some delicious berries unobtainable in Europe, our greatest loss is the lack of the fabulous fish and shellfish which abounds, particularly off the west coast. Abalone, black bass, cioppino, clam and tuna as well as a prolific supply of crab, lobster and Pacific salmon, provide a richness and variety of seafood that Europeans do not enjoy.

The delights of many of these sea creatures are forbidden to the Muslims

215

of Persia and India and those fish which they are allowed to eat have been nearly impossible to obtain except right on the coast. The cooking of Persia and India relies almost exclusively, therefore, on meat for the main dishes. As may be expected they are full of aromatic spices and the flavourings tend to be subtle, with a blend of three or four spices for each dish, rather than a mass of conflicting flavours resulting in the rather hot taste that ready-made curry powders tend to give. The desserts have not changed for centuries, and are what we should describe as sweetmeats rather than puddings. Sweet loaves dipped in syrup, scented with rose-water or orange flower water, and rolled in scented sugar are found in El Baghdadi's fourteenth-century manual of cooking, and this and many other traditional dishes can be found in modern books on Middle East cookery today.

Some readers may wonder why there are no veal dishes since many of the old books included recipes for veal. The omission is intentional. Apart from the horrifying conditions under which veal is produced today which prompt many people to eschew it as a matter of principle, modern veal bears no resemblance to that of the past. The almost tasteless, dry white meat from artificially fed calves is quite unlike the succulent flesh obtained from the slowly reared young animals that fed on fresh milk and natural fodder in the days preceding factory farming, and the old recipes for veal would be impossible to reproduce using the modern variety.

Greek and Roman Recipes

In order to follow the recipes faithfully one should have a small supply of coriander, oregano, cumin and caraway as well as thyme, parsley and mint. A few of the more unusual herbs are needed: lovage, rue and savory as well as pine kernels which can be bought at branches of Culpeper House, some health food shops and delicatessens as well as specialist herb-growers. The Romans had no sugar and never cooked with butter, so honey was used for sweetening and lots of olive oil and wine went into their dishes.

Passum was specially sweetened wine and where mentioned a cheap sweet white wine in which a few raisins have been soaked or with a little honey added is a good substitute.

Defrutum, also mentioned, was prepared from must and new wine and a substitute can be achieved by pressing the juice from some grapes and boiling it up to reduce a little. It adds a subtle flavour to a dish.

Finally, no Roman recipe is complete without *garum* or *liquamen*, the words are interchangeable, which was the seasoning they used instead of salt. The *Geoponica* describes how factory-made *garum* was produced, involving a lengthy process of drying fish in the sun, but luckily it also mentions a quick method for small households which tells us to make brine and test its strength by floating an egg in it, then fish such as sprats, mullet, mackerel or anchovies were boiled in the brine until it began to reduce. Flavourings of oregano and *defrutum* were sometimes added, then the liquid was cooled, strained two or three times until it was clear, sealed and stored away. If you cannot be bothered to make the experiment, then use salt to taste in the usual way, but the salty liquid *garum* distributes its taste very evenly and harmoniously and can be used in any dish requiring salt, not just a Roman dish. Here is a simple way of making it which will keep for weeks.

GARUM
½ lb kitchen salt
1½ pints water
6 tinned anchovy fillets

1 level teaspoon oregano
6 tablespoons defrutum

Stir the salt into the water until it dissolves. Pour into a saucepan and add the anchovies, oregano and grape juice, if used. Bring to the boil, and cook briskly for 15 minutes. Cool, strain through muslin three or four times until the liquid is free of bits and fairly clear. When cold, bottle, or keep in a screw-topped jar.

About 2–3 teaspoons of *garum* are equal in strength to ¼ teaspoon dry salt for seasoning.

GASTRIS – according to Chrysippus

Sweetened nut cakes such as these were eaten in ancient Greece much as they are in Greece today. They would have been eaten at the end of a meal with wine.

MAKES 24 PIECES
2 oz shelled hazelnuts　　　　　　　*¼ lb thick honey*
2 oz shelled walnuts　　　　　　　　*2 oz sesame seeds*
4 oz blanched almonds　　　　　　　*poppy seeds*

Place all the nuts in a tin and roast in a hot oven, watching carefully, until toasted brown. Grind them thoroughly through a parsley mill or nut grater so that they are fairly coarse, and put them in a bowl.

Place the honey in a saucepan and bring to the boil. Draw off the heat and cool slightly. Add sufficient honey to the ground nuts to make a soft mass. With floured hands, shape the mixture into two flattish round 'cakes'.

Grind the sesame seeds and mix with the remaining honey to obtain a mixture of the same consistency. Shape and flatten in the same manner to a 'cake' of similar size. Sprinkle top and sides with poppy seeds and gently press in. Sandwich the sesame seed mixture between the two layers of nut mixture and press together.

Store for two days before serving to allow mixture to firm up. Then cut into pieces. This nut cake will easily keep a week.

Athenaeus: *The Deipnosophists*

IN OVIS HEPALIS

SOFT BOILED EGGS

This is a most delicious and unusual dish. It makes the perfect starter for a lunch party. Pine kernels are really necessary in this recipe for the very subtle flavour they give to the sauce. The eggs are soft boiled, shelled and eaten cold with the sauce, which has the consistency of mayonnaise.

SERVES 4
4 eggs　　　　　　　　　　　　　　*1½ tablespoons white wine vinegar*
3 oz pine kernels, soaked overnight　　*1 teaspoon garum*
¼ level teaspoon ground lovage　　　*freshly milled black pepper*
¼ teaspoon honey

Put the eggs into boiling water and simmer for 5 minutes. Plunge into cold water and leave for 8 minutes. Carefully peel away the shells and keep the eggs submerged in cold water until ready for use.

Put the pine kernels into an electric liquidizer (the Romans used slaves and a pestle and mortar) and blend to a creamy consistency. Pour into a bowl and stir in the lovage, honey and wine vinegar. Add the *garum* and plenty of freshly milled black pepper. Stir until thoroughly mixed.

Serve the eggs in a shallow dish with the sauce spooned over. This is nice eaten with brown bread and butter.

Apicius: *De Re Coquinaria*

PATINA SOLEARUM

PATINA OF SOLES

This sauce, in which either fillets or small whole fish are cooked, is a most delicate complement to the naturally good flavour of fresh sole.

SERVES 4

4 small Dover sole or about 1½ lb filleted sole	*1 level teaspoon ground lovage*
3 tablespoons olive oil	*2 heaped teaspoons oregano*
2 teaspoons garum	*¼ level teaspoon ground pepper*
¼ pint dry white wine	*1 large or 2 small eggs*

Clean and skin the soles if whole fish are used. Place the fish in a shallow saucepan with the oil, *garum* and wine. Cover and poach gently for 10–15 minutes until the fish is cooked, then draw off the heat.

Put the lovage, oregano and pepper into a bowl with 3 tablespoons of the liquid in which the fish has cooked. Stir in the lightly mixed egg. Slowly pour this mixture over the fish in the pan. Return the pan to a low heat and bring slowly to the boil. Stir occasionally to keep the sauce smooth and simmer for about 10 minutes.

Spoon the fish and sauce into a hot serving dish, sprinkle with a little freshly milled pepper and serve.

Apicius: *De Re Coquinaria*

IUS IN PISCE ASSO

SAUCE FOR GRILLED FISH

This sauce would go very well with grilled halibut. The flavour is piquant with wine and vinegar, which the honey saves from being too sharp, and nicely aromatic with herbs. It has a clean and refreshing taste which would not overburden even the most delicate fish.

SUFFICIENT FOR 4 SERVINGS

2 rounded teaspoons chopped thyme	*3 tablespoons white wine vinegar*
1 level teaspoon ground lovage	*3 teaspoons garum*
1 level teaspoon ground coriander	*4 tablespoons olive oil*
¼ level teaspoon ground black pepper	*1 tablespoon defrutum (pressed grape juice)*
2 teaspoons honey	*1 rounded teaspoon cornflour*

Place the thyme, lovage, coriander, black pepper, honey, vinegar, white wine, *garum*, olive oil and grape juice in a saucepan and warm gently. Blend the cornflour with a little water and stir into the ingredients. Bring up to the boil, stirring all the time until the sauce thickens.

Serve with any grilled fish.

Apicius: *De Re Coquinaria*

LUCUSTAS ASSAS

GRILLED CRAYFISH

For this recipe the crayfish should really be raw, then split in half. They are cooked under the grill and basted with a coriander sauce throughout the cooking time to keep the flesh from drying out. If you use the crayfish or lobster that has already been boiled, then they will only need 5–6 minutes under the grill with the sauce poured over them whenever they begin to look dry. The sauce has a subtle, sharp flavour which perfectly sets off the shellfish.

SERVES 2
1 crayfish or large lobster

FOR THE SAUCE

2 rounded teaspoons ground coriander
2 level teaspoons ground lovage
½ level teaspoon ground caraway
¼ level teaspoon ground black pepper
4 finely chopped dates
1 teaspoon honey

2 tablespoons white wine vinegar
2 tablespoons dry white wine
3 teaspoons garum
3 tablespoons olive oil
2 tablespoons defrutum *(pressed grape juice)*

Split the crayfish in half and remove the lungs which are found in the head section.

Place the coriander, lovage, caraway, pepper and dates in a bowl. Add the honey, vinegar, wine, *garum*, olive oil and grape juice. Blend thoroughly, making sure that the dates are evenly mixed through. Spoon a little of the sauce over the crayfish or lobster flesh and set under a hot grill. Keep basting with more sauce until the flesh is cooked – takes 15–20 minutes. Or if they are previously boiled, until thoroughly heated through. Serve hot.

Apicius: *De Re Coquinaria*

AD AVES OMNI GENERE

BIRD IN PASTE

Nothing could be more succulent than this method of cooking a chicken wrapped in a flour and oil paste. All the juices and flavour of the chicken are retained.

SERVES 4
1 fresh chicken, about 3¼ lb dressed weight *little olive oil*

FOR THE PASTE
1½ lb plain flour *½–¾ pint olive oil*

Wipe the chicken and then brush all over with olive oil. Set aside while preparing the flour and oil paste.

Sift the flour into a bowl and stir in the oil, mixing well to make a soft dough. Turn out on to a floured working surface and divide the dough into two unequal parts. Press the smaller piece out with the hands, slightly larger than the chicken all round. Lay the chicken in the centre. Press out the larger piece and drape it over the bird. Press the edges well together to completely seal the chicken inside the paste. Lightly oil a roasting tin and place the chicken on it. Set in the centre of a moderately hot oven (375 deg. F or Gas No. 5) and bake the bird for 2¼ hours. The addition of a paste jacket considerably increases the baking time.

When the cooking time is complete, break open the crust and lift out the bird. Serve with the following sauce.

IUS CANDIDUM IN AVEM ELIXAM

WHITE SAUCE FOR A BIRD

This piquant white sauce should be served sparingly like mustard or mint sauce. It is also good cold. Almonds, hazelnuts or walnuts can be used.

SUFFICIENT FOR 4 SERVINGS

2 oz blanched almonds	2 teaspoons garum
½ level teaspoon ground pepper	1 teaspoon honey
½ level teaspoon ground lovage	2 tablespoons olive oil
1 level teaspoon ground cumin	3 tablespoons white wine vinegar
1 level teaspoon celery seed	

Lightly toast the almonds and grind them coarsely into a bowl. Add the pepper, lovage, cumin, celery seed, the *garum* and honey. Stir in the oil and vinegar. At this stage the mixture should be fairly runny as the nuts will absorb the liquid. Pour into a small saucepan and simmer very gently for 10 minutes. Draw off the heat and allow to stand in a warm place for 30 minutes.

Reheat gently just before serving.

Apicius: *De Re Coquinaria*

HAEDUM SIVE AGNUM PARTHICUM

KID OR LAMB THE PARTHIAN WAY

This sauce which accompanies roast lamb tastes spicy sweet, rather like a good mild chutney. The original recipe used damsons which, if obtainable, would be simply delicious as would any cooking plum. When fresh fruit is not obtainable, use prunes first simmered in a little red wine until they are tender.

SERVES 6

shoulder of lamb, about 4 lb in weight	oil for roasting

10 cooking plums or 10 cooked prunes　　　　*2 level teaspoons marjoram or savory*
2 onions　　　　　　　　　　　　　　　　　*3 teaspoons garum*
3 tablespoons olive oil　　　　　　　　　　*½ pint red wine*
½ teaspoon ground pepper　　　　　　　　*1 tablespoon white wine vinegar*
3 level teaspoons rue

Roast the lamb with a little oil in the roasting tin in a moderately hot oven (375 deg. F or Gas No. 5) for 1¾ hours or until nicely brown and crisp on the outside.

Meanwhile prepare the sauce. Stone the plums or prunes and chop roughly. Peel and chop the onions. Heat the oil in a saucepan, add the onions and fry gently until soft. Add the pepper, rue, marjoram, *garum*, plums or prunes and wine. Cook gently for about 15 minutes. Just before serving add the vinegar.

Hand the sauce separately in a sauce-boat, or carve the meat on to a hot dish and spoon the sauce over.

Apicius: *De Re Coquinaria*

PERNA

HAM

When ham, or gammon, is boiled with dried figs it acquires a wonderful flavour. If you want to follow this recipe exactly you must finish cooking the ham in a paste covering made from flour and olive oil. This keeps the flesh beautifully moist, but the oil is expensive (since you do not eat the crust) and you can still achieve a fine honey-baked ham by simply glazing the joint in the oven. Any left over is delicious cold.

SERVES 6–8

5 lb piece of gammon, soaked in cold water　　*3 bay leaves*
　　for several hours　　　　　　　　　　　*2 tablespoons honey*
½ lb dried figs

Flour and oil paste, see page 220.

Drain the soaked gammon and rinse well. Place in a large saucepan with the figs and bay leaves and add fresh cold water to cover. Bring to the boil and simmer for 1½ hours.

Lift the gammon from the pan, drain well and allow to cool for a few moments. Using a sharp knife carefully remove the rind. Make criss-cross incisions in the fat and spread the honey over the surface so the cuts are filled.

Roll out the flour and oil paste, place the gammon in the centre and wrap the dough around pressing the edges well together to seal the gammon inside. Place on an oiled baking tray. Set in a moderately hot oven (375 deg. F or Gas No. 5) and bake for 45 minutes. Break the crust open to remove the gammon and serve hot.

Note: If you want to omit the paste, about 30 minutes baking in a moderately hot oven will be enough to brown and glaze the surface.

Apicius: *De Re Coquinaria*

SUCKING PIG COOKED IN A METAL CASSEROLE

This method of roasting pork is so delicious that if you cook no other Roman recipe I recommend you try this one. Pork roasted any other way will afterwards seem dull in comparison. The original recipe is for sucking-pig, but a good loin of pork cooks into an aromatic and succulent dish. The recipe tells us to cook the pig in a metal pan, a self-basting roasting tin is ideal.

SERVES 6

3 tablespoons olive oil
1 loin of pork, about 4½ lb with the rind on
½ pint red wine
¼ pint water

2 dessertspoons garum
1 heaped teaspoon ground coriander
1 leek
6 tablespoons defrutum *(pressed grape juice)*

FOR THE SAUCE

½ level teaspoon ground pepper
½ level teaspoon ground lovage
½ level teaspoon ground caraway
½ level teaspoon ground celery seed

1 level teaspoon oregano
3 tablespoons passum *(sweet white wine)*
3 tablespoons red wine
1 level tablespoon cornflour

Heat the oil in a metal casserole or self-basting roasting tin over direct heat. Place in the pork and brown gently on all sides. Add the red wine, the water and half the *garum*. Add the coriander and the leek, well washed and sliced in half lengthwise. Cover and place in a hot oven (400 deg. F or Gas No. 6) and cook allowing 25 minutes per lb and 25 minutes extra. Half-way through the cooking time, pour the grape juice over the pork and lower the temperature to moderately hot (375 deg. F or Gas No. 5) if the pork is browning too fast.

Place the pepper, lovage, caraway, celery seed and oregano into a saucepan. Add the rest of the *garum*, the sweet white wine, the red wine and 3 tablespoons of the liquid in which the pork is cooking. Bring to the boil and simmer together for 15 minutes. Draw off the heat and set aside.

Dish up the pork and pour off some of the fat remaining in the casserole or roasting tin. Blend the cornflour with a little cold water and then stir into the mixture in the saucepan. Tip the contents of the pan into the juices in the roasting tin. Bring up to the boil stirring all the time until the mixture thickens. Serve separately in a sauce-boat with a grinding of black pepper added.

Apicius: *De Re Coquinaria*

IUS IN COPADIIS

SAUCE FOR COLD MEAT

This is described in the old recipe as a sauce for cold meat slices, and it is a very good enlivener of any left-over cold joint. Carve the meat and arrange on a dish, then spoon the sweet-sour sauce generously over the slices. The original recipe included aromatic black myrtle berries. One or two berries crushed and added to the other herbs gave distinction to the flavour. But the sauce is good without them.

3 hard-boiled eggs

1 medium or 2 small leeks

½ level teaspoon ground cumin

1 level teaspoon ground black pepper

1 heaped tablespoon chopped parsley

2 teaspoons honey

2 teaspoons garum

1 tablespoon white wine vinegar

3 tablespoons olive oil

Shell the hard-boiled eggs and chop them finely. Trim the leeks, discarding most of the green part. Cut into pieces and cook in boiling water for 15 minutes. Then drain and chop finely.

Place the cumin, pepper, parsley, chopped eggs and leeks in a bowl. Add the honey, *garum*, vinegar and oil. Stir well and spoon the sauce over the sliced cold meat.

Apicius: *De Re Coquinaria*

HAEDEM SIVE AGNNAMEX CALDATUM

HOT KID OR LAMB STEW

Quite a cheap cut such as best end neck of lamb is ideal for this tender stew, fragrant with herbs and wine. It is simple to prepare and can be kept hot without spoiling.

SERVES 4

2 pieces best end neck of lamb, total weight about 3 lb

1 large onion

1 rounded teaspoon ground coriander

freshly milled black pepper

½ level teaspoon ground cumin

2 level teaspoons ground lovage

½ pint dry white wine

3 tablespoons olive oil

3 teaspoons garum

1 rounded teaspoon cornflour

Trim surplus fat from the lamb and cut the meat into neat pieces. Peel and finely chop the onion. Place the lamb pieces and the onion into a saucepan. Add the coriander, a good seasoning of freshly milled black pepper, the cumin and lovage. Pour in the white wine, add the olive oil and the *garum*. Bring slowly to the boil, then cover and simmer gently for 1¼ hours.

Lift out the lamb pieces and keep warm. Strain the gravy into a saucepan and reserve the onion and herb pieces retained in the sieve. Blend the cornflour with a little cold water. Add a small amount of the gravy, mix well and pour into the rest of the gravy in the saucepan. Bring up to the boil stirring until the mixture has thickened. Tip in the onion and the herb contents from the sieve and heat through.

Pour over the meat and serve.

Apicius: *De Re Coquinaria*

MINUTAL EX PRAECOQUIS

FRICASSEE WITH APRICOTS

In this recipe a piece of pork is first roasted then diced and cooked with apricots, spices and wine until it is reduced to a tender fricassee consistency. The Romans sometimes used crumbled pastry to thicken their sauces and gravies. It works perfectly well and leaves no taste. One could use a crumbled Weetabix, plain crushed biscuit or even a little coarse wholemeal flour without noticeably altering the dish, which is full of the flavour of spices and herbs.

SERVES 4–6

1 piece leg of pork, about 3½ lb	*1 level teaspoon ground cumin*
3 shallots or 1 small onion	*1 level teaspoon dried mint*
4 tablespoons olive oil	*2 level teaspoons dried dill*
½ pint dry white wine	*3 teaspoons honey*
4 teaspoons garum	*2 teaspoons* garum
¼ lb fresh apricots, or dried apricots	*2 tablespoons white wine vinegar*
soaked overnight	*1 tablespoon passum (sweet white wine)*
¼ level teaspoon ground black pepper	*piece of pastry or biscuit*

Set the pork in an oiled roasting tin and place in a moderately hot oven (375 deg. F or Gas No. 5) and roast allowing 25 minutes per lb and 25 minutes extra. Remove from the tin, cut the roasted pork into dice and place in a saucepan. Peel and chop the shallots and add to the pork along with the oil, wine and *garum*. Cook gently for 30 minutes. Halve and stone the fresh apricots. If using dried apricots, simmer the soaked fruit in a little water for 30 minutes or until tender, then drain.

Place the black pepper, cumin, mint, dill, honey, *garum*, vinegar and sweet white wine into a bowl. Add ¼ pint of the cooking liquor from the pork. Mix well and return to the saucepan in which the pork is cooking. Add the apricots and continue to simmer gently, covered with a lid, for a further 1¼ hours until all the ingredients are very tender. About 5 minutes before serving stir in some crumbled pastry (about the size of a small saucer), a Weetabix or a plain biscuit. Stir to thicken the gravy and serve.

Apicius: *De Re Coquinaria*

GRUEM VEL ANATEM

SAUCE FOR ROAST DUCK OR CRANE

When you read the ingredients for this sauce to be served with roast duck (or crane as the original suggested) you will probably be thoroughly put off. Indeed so was I until the minced chicken livers went in at the end, the oil was absorbed and the combined flavours blended into their final form which was wonderful with roast duck. I was reminded again that the Romans were masters of the art of making sauces, and that these old recipes offer us a fascinating original composition of flavours.

SERVES 4

3 oz chicken livers	*½ level teaspoon oregano*
1 tablespoon olive oil	*2 teaspoons* garum
½ cucumber	*1 level teaspoon honey*
1 rounded teaspoon ground lovage	*1 tablespoon white wine vinegar*
¼ level teaspoon freshly ground black pepper	*2 tablespoons olive oil*

Trim the chicken livers and fry lightly in the tablespoon of olive oil. Drain and chop finely. Peel and slice the cucumber thinly, cook in boiling water for 10 minutes, then drain well.

Place the lovage, pepper, oregano and *garum* into a small saucepan. Add the honey, vinegar and oil. Bring to the boil, stir and cook for 3–4 minutes. Add the sliced cucumber and the chopped chicken livers. Stir well and simmer for a further 5 minutes. Pour into a warmed sauce-boat, add a little freshly ground black pepper and serve with roast duck.

Apicius: *De Re Coquinaria*

INTUBA

ENDIVE

The Romans used both endive and chicory in their recipes. They used the same word for both, much as we do today, so it is not always clear which one was intended. However, the following dressing with a little chopped raw onion is delicate with sliced raw chicory as a winter salad.

SERVES 4

4 heads of chicory	*1 tablespoon olive oil*
1 small onion	*1 tablespoon dry white wine*
2 teaspoons garum	

Wash the chicory and slice across into rounds. Peel and finely chop the onion. Mix the two together and dress with the *garum*, oil and wine.

Apicius: *De Re Coquinaria*

PISAM

PEAS

For years the British cook has been criticized for cooking her vegetables with bicarbonate of soda to keep them green. It is amusing to learn from Apicius that back in Roman times they used *nitrum* or potassium nitrate to keep the colour. It has the same effect as the despised bicarbonate of soda.

Make this dish with fresh or dried peas. It is very good served as an *hors d'œuvre*, or as a vegetable with cold meats. This is one of the few recipes in which dry salt was used instead of *garum*.

SERVES 4

½ lb dried peas, soaked overnight	*2½ tablespoons olive oil*
½ level teaspoon bicarbonate of soda	*1 dessertspoon white wine vinegar*
1 small onion	*1 teaspoon salt*
2 hard-boiled eggs	

Drain the peas and place in a saucepan. Re-cover with fresh cold water and add the bicarbonate of soda. Bring up to the boil and simmer for 45 minutes or until the peas are tender. Strain and leave until cold.

Peel and finely chop the onion. Cut the hard-boiled eggs in half and tip out the yolks. Finely chop the egg white. Mix the onion and egg white with the peas. Dress the mixture with the oil, vinegar and salt. Press the egg yolks through a sieve on top of the peas. Sprinkle with a little more olive oil and serve.

Apicius: *De Re Coquinaria*

PORROS

LEEKS

Serve this unusual recipe for leeks hot or cold. For a hot vegetable it is advisable to return the dressed leeks and butter beans to the pan and heat them through together before serving.

SERVES 4

6 oz butter beans, soaked overnight
1½ lb leeks
3 tablespoons olive oil

2 teaspoons garum
2½ tablespoons dry white wine

Drain the soaked butter beans and place in a saucepan. Re-cover with fresh cold water, bring up to the boil and simmer for 45 minutes or until tender. Then drain well.

Trim and wash the leeks. Cook in boiling water for 15 minutes or until tender. Drain well and place in a serving dish. Dress with the olive oil, *garum* and the wine. Stir in the butter beans.

Apicius: *De Re Coquinaria*

BOLETUS

MUSHROOMS

If boletus are not obtainable, cultivated or field mushrooms make a good dish and take only a few minutes cooking time.

This mushroom dish makes a nice starter and is good either hot or cold. It would be especially interesting as part of a mixed hors d'œuvre.

SERVES 2–4

½ lb boletus, or field mushrooms
¼ level teaspoon ground black pepper
½ level teaspoon ground lovage

1 teaspoon honey
1 teaspoon garum
2 tablespoons olive oil

Slice the mushrooms and place in a shallow saucepan. Add the pepper, lovage, honey, *garum* and olive oil. Cook gently for 40 minutes if boletus, or 5 minutes if field mushrooms until just tender, but not soft.

Serve hot or cold.

Apicius: *De Re Coquinaria*

TYROPATINAM

MILK AND EGG SWEET

There are hardly any written recipes for Roman desserts, but this one explains quite clearly how to strain the milk and egg mixture into an earthenware pot and cook over a slow fire until set. This suggests it was not stirred over direct heat but allowed to set in a slow oven. The sprinkling of pepper gives a slightly aromatic flavour, not unlike the nutmeg we would use today.

SERVES 4–6
1 pint milk
1 tablespoon honey

4–5 eggs
pinch ground white pepper

Warm the milk and honey and stir to blend. Crack the eggs into a mixing bowl and gradually whisk in the warm milk and honey. Strain into a 1½–2 pint earthenware baking dish. Set in the centre of a slow oven (300 deg. F or Gas No. 2) and bake for 1½–2 hours or until the custard has set. Sprinkle with a pinch of pepper and serve warm or cold.

Apicius: *De Re Coquinaria*

Medieval Recipes

As with the Roman *garum*, Medieval cooking requires the use of almond milk. This was much esteemed and although now lost to Western cooking it is still made in the Middle East, where it is diluted with ice-cold water and taken as a refreshing drink. Simple instructions for making it from ground almonds and water are given below. Sometimes the instructions are to make it 'chargeaunt', or stiff, and sometimes 'rynning'. Sometimes it was made with wine or broth, instead of water, but not, however, with milk as its name suggests. The almond flavour adds a delicate fragrance to sauces, whether savoury or sweet.

ALMOND MILK

4 oz ground almonds   ½ pint water

Tie the almonds loosely in a piece of muslin. Pour the cold water into a basin and soak the almonds in this for several hours, occasionally shaking and squeezing the muslin until all the white 'milk' has been extracted.

To make a thicker milk, the almonds may be gently simmered in water for 10 minutes and then pressed through a food mill to make a purée.

Saffron, pine kernels, garlic, cardamoms and verjuice are some of the more exotic flavourings used in Medieval cookery. Verjuice was a sharp brew of crab-apples or sour grapes and used in cooking as we use lemon juice, which is a very good substitute for verjuice. In order to preserve the verjuice during the many months between the crab-apple season and the appearance of sour grapes, it is very probable that it was fermented. If you wish it is quite easy to make a very 'dry' wine from crab-apples that can be stored and used as required.

CRUSTARDES OF EERBIS ON FYSSH DAY

The marvellous thing about this recipe is that by baking quite ordinary fish in the pastry case, a firm texture and crisp flavour results in something very like shellfish. Half-way through the cooking time 'the sewe', or sauce is added and this mixture of herbs and walnuts puts the finishing touch to a fish dish that can stand alone as the main course, or make a perfect supper dish. The original recipe used verjuice, that medieval brew of sour green grapes or crab-apples, with 'as myche wat' (water). But lemon juice is a good substitute. Use what herbs you have to hand and to your taste, 'gode Eerbs' are all that are specified.

6 oz shortcrust pastry
1¼ lb fresh haddock
salt and black pepper

pinch ground cinnamon
2 tablespoons olive oil

FOR THE SAUCE MIXTURE
2 oz shelled walnuts
bunch fresh parsley
2 sprigs fresh thyme
2 sprigs fresh lemon balm

1 small sprig fresh rosemary
juice of 1 lemon and the same quantity of water
generous pinch of saffron

Roll out the pastry and line an 8–9-inch pie plate and set aside. Using a sharp knife, remove and discard the skin of the fish. Chop the flesh in rough pieces and fill the pastry case with the fish. Season well with salt and pepper and a pinch of cinnamon. Spoon over the oil. Place in the centre of a moderate oven (350 deg. F or Gas No. 4) and bake for 20 minutes.

Meanwhile prepare the sauce mixture. Blanch the walnuts in boiling water for 2 minutes. Remove them one at a time and peel off as much of the brown skin as possible, using a sharp knife. Chop the walnuts. Wash and strip the herbs from their stalks, chop coarsely or pass through a parsley mill and place in a saucepan with the walnuts. Add the lemon juice, water and saffron. Season with pepper. Simmer the ingredients all together for 5 minutes, then draw off the heat.

Spoon the sauce mixture over the top of the partly baked fish. Return to the oven and bake for a further 10 minutes.

Serve hot.

The Forme of Cury, about 1390

MORTREWYS DE FLEYSSH

This pork dish results in a rich and subtly flavoured hash. A recipe that could be served as a main course, or used for a starter, like pâté, and served with hot toast.

SERVES 4
2 lb spare rib of pork
1 pint pale ale
1 pint water
4 tablespoons fresh breadcrumbs

pinch saffron strands,
*   soaked in 2 tablespoons of hot water*
salt to taste
2 egg yolks
generous pinch ground ginger

Place the pork in a saucepan with the ale and the water. Bring to the boil and skim. Cover the pan and allow to simmer for 2 hours. Lift out the pork, remove the skin and any small bones. Reserve the cooking broth.

Finely chop or mince the cooked pork and place in a clean saucepan. Place the bread-crumbs in a bowl and add ¼ pint of the reserved broth. Allow the crumbs to soak for a few minutes, then sieve the mixture into the pan with the meat. Add the saffron and stir in sufficient of the meat broth to make a soft, but not wet, mixture. Add salt to taste and place the pan over a low heat. When thoroughly heated through, but not boiling, stir in the egg yolks. Stir for a further few minutes until the mixture is thick, then draw off the heat.

Serve hot with a generous sprinkling of ground ginger on top.

Potage Dyvers, about 1420

MONCHELET

'Caste thereto erbes yhewe, gode wyne and a qntite of oynons mynced, powder fort and saffron and alye (allay) it with ayrens (eggs) and Verjuice.' 'Powder fort' was powdered ginger and pepper and any of the stronger-flavoured spices, as opposed to 'powder douce' which was a combination of milder flavours. The individual herbs were not specified, the choice was left to the cook and what was available in the garden. The exact quantities were always omitted from these early recipes, but the resulting sauce should be aromatic and spicy and of a delicious golden colour.

SERVES 4

2 lb middle neck of lamb, cut in pieces	pinch saffron
1 pint stock	pinch ground ginger
2 heaped tablespoons fresh mint	¼ level teaspoon ground cinnamon
1 teaspoon fresh thyme	salt and pepper
1 sprig fresh marjoram	2 egg yolks
4 small or 2 large onions	1 tablespoon lemon juice
½ pint dry white wine	

Trim away any surplus fat and place the pieces of meat in a large saucepan. Add the stock, the chopped mint, thyme and marjoram, the peeled and chopped onions and the wine. Add the saffron, ginger and cinnamon and a seasoning of salt and pepper. Cover and simmer gently for 1½ hours. Lift the meat out of the pan and keep warm in a deep serving dish.

Blend the egg yolks with a little of the hot broth taken from the pan. Return the mixture to the pan and stir over a gentle heat until it thickens. Draw off the heat and stir in the lemon juice to sharpen the flavour. Pour over the meat and serve.

The Forme of Cury, about 1390

CAPOUN OR GOS FARCED

Although the original recipe is for capon or goose, the size of either bird is extravagantly large to stuff with grapes, even though it does say 'for defawte of grapis, oynons fyrst wil y-boylid and alle to-chopped' may be used. The tender whole grapes with their seasonings make a wonderful stuffing for any roast chicken. Onions as a substitute would not be nearly so unusual.

SERVES 6

1 chicken, about 4–4½ lb

FOR THE STUFFING

½ lb lean pork	¼ level teaspoon ground ginger
4 whole cloves	¼ level teaspoon ground cinnamon
3 hard-boiled egg yolks	¼ level teaspoon pepper
¼ lb fresh suet	¼ level teaspoon salt
2 heaped tablespoons chopped fresh parsley	½ lb seedless green grapes
1 level teaspoon powdered saffron	

Wipe the chicken and set aside while preparing the stuffing. Parboil the pork for about 15 minutes, then drain and leave until cool enough to handle. Cut in pieces and pass through the mincer with the cloves. Using a wooden spoon, cream the hard-boiled egg yolks and then add the grated suet, chopped parsley, saffron, ginger, cinnamon and salt and pepper. Blend the two mixtures well and then add the whole grapes.

Use this mixture to stuff the body cavity of the chicken. Secure the tail skin. Place in a roasting tin with some dripping and cover with well-greased kitchen foil. Set in the centre of a moderately hot oven (375 deg. F or Gas No. 5) and roast for 1 hour 40 minutes. Remove the foil towards the end of the cooking time.

Leche Vyaundez, 1430

ALOWS DE BEEF OR DE MOTOUN

This dish is possibly the origin of beef olives. The stuffing is smooth in texture, slightly spicy and very green from the chopped parsley. The original says 'putte hem on a round spete and roste hem till they ben y-naw'. With an oven-spit you can do this, otherwise they can be laid in a greased or oiled roasting tin and baked.

SERVES 4

4 thin slices topside of beef	*1 rounded teaspoon saffron strands, soaked*
2 medium onions	*in 2 tablespoons hot water*
½ oz lard	*or 1 level teaspoon powdered saffron*
4 hard-boiled egg yolks	*1 level teaspoon ground ginger*
2 oz fresh suet	*½ level teaspoon salt*
a bunch of fresh parsley	

FOR THE SAUCE

2 hard-boiled egg yolks	*¼ level teaspoon ground ginger*
juice of ½ lemon	*¼ level teaspoon ground cinnamon*
4 tablespoons wine vinegar	*¼ level teaspoon pepper*

Beat out the steaks to flatten them. Set aside while preparing the stuffing. Peel and finely chop the onions and fry in the lard for a few minutes until tender but not brown. Finely chop the hard-boiled egg yolks and grate the suet. Wash and finely chop the parsley. Combine the onion, chopped egg yolks, suet and parsley together in a bowl. Add the infused saffron and ginger and mix thoroughly together.

Divide the mixture equally and spread on each of the 4 steaks. Season with salt and roll up neatly. Secure with fine string or a cocktail stick and place in an oiled or greased roasting tin. Set in a very moderate oven (325 deg. F or Gas No. 3) and bake for 30 minutes or until the steaks are done.

Meanwhile prepare the sauce. Using a wooden spoon, cream the egg yolks with the lemon juice in a basin. Stir in the vinegar, ginger, cinnamon and pepper. Heat the mixture through gently in a small saucepan. Taste, and if the flavour is a little too sharp for your liking, add a teaspoon of sugar and the two hard-boiled egg whites, finely chopped.

Dish up the steaks. Spoon a little of the piquant sauce on the side of each plate, or hand separately.

Potage Dyvers, about 1420

In the Middle Ages breadcrumbs seem to have been used to thicken sauces and stews in the same way as we would use flour. The Romans sometimes used crumbled pastry for the same purpose. The original of this recipe tells us to 'stepe faire brede with the same broth' (that would be the broth in which the rabbit cooked) and proceeds to 'drawe' it through a 'straynour' with 'vinegre'. This really does work and thickens the liquid without leaving any trace of breadcrumbs. The resulting fragrant white sauce, which is not too strong tasting, would be equally good with chicken and excellent for a boiling fowl. Either could be used in place of the rabbit in this recipe.

SERVES 4

1 rabbit, or 2 lb rabbit pieces	*generous ½ pint dry white wine*
1 bay leaf	*6 whole cloves*
1 blade mace	*2 blades mace*
juice ½ lemon	*½ level teaspoon ground cinnamon*
½ oz lard	*salt and pepper*
½ oz dripping	*2 oz fresh breadcrumbs*
2 large onions	*2 tablespoons white wine vinegar*
generous ½ pint stock	*pinch ground ginger*

Place the rabbit pieces in a basin and cover with cold salted water. Add the bay leaf, mace and a squeeze of lemon juice. Leave to soak overnight.

Drain the rabbit pieces and pat them dry. Heat the lard and dripping in a large heavy saucepan. Add the rabbit pieces to the hot fat and fry gently to brown them on all sides. Remove the pieces from the pan and keep hot. Peel and finely chop the onions and add to the hot fat remaining in the pan. Fry gently for a few minutes until tender and beginning to brown. Then return the pieces of rabbit and add the stock and wine. Together they should be sufficient to cover the rabbit pieces. Add the cloves, mace, cinnamon and a seasoning of salt and plenty of freshly ground pepper. Cover and simmer gently for 1 hour.

Place the breadcrumbs in a bowl and mix about ⅓ pint (approximately 1 teacupful) of the hot broth from the rabbit. Pass through a sieve into a small saucepan. Bring up to the boil and then return the mixture to the pan with the rabbit, adding a pinch of ginger. Re-cover the pan and allow to cook for a further 30 minutes. Check seasoning and serve.

Potage Dyvers, about 1420

BLANC MANG

This makes a delicious savoury dish of chicken and rice 'flourished' (garnished) with 'Almandes fryed in oyle'. There is an even earlier medieval version of this dish called a *Blanc Manger* in a collection of German crusader recipes and this was made as a sweet using almond milk, plucked chicken breasts, rice flour and sugar. In the Middle East a sweet is still made using only the pounded white breasts of chicken flavoured with sugar and almonds, so it would seem that this dish originated in the Middle East and was brought to Europe by the returning Crusaders. We would find it strange to use flesh, even as bland as chicken, in a sweet, yet this English medieval dish may have been served as one, since no exact quantities of sugar are given in the recipe.

SERVES 6

1 boiling chicken 5½–6 lb
2 bay leaves
6 peppercorns
1½ level teaspoons salt
3 oz ground almonds

3 oz long grain rice
1 rounded teaspoon sugar
3 oz flaked almonds
olive oil for frying

Put the chicken in a large saucepan with enough cold water to reach about half way up the bird. Add the bay leaves, peppercorns and 1 level teaspoon of the salt. Bring to the boil, skim and simmer gently for 2 hours or until tender. Lift out the chicken and allow to cool. Put the ground almonds into a basin and strain over them ½ pint of the hot chicken broth taken from the pan. Stir well to make an almond-flavoured broth and set aside.

Wash the rice and stir it into the pan of chicken broth. Bring to the boil and cook for 12 minutes until the rice is just tender. Drain the rice and set aside.

Take the chicken flesh off the bone. Discard the skin and cut the flesh into bite-sized pieces. Place in a saucepan with the almond-flavoured broth, the remaining ½ teaspoon of salt and the sugar. Heat through, then add the cooked rice and stir all together until mixed and well heated. Fry the flaked almonds in olive oil until golden brown.

Dish the chicken and rice, and garnish with the fried almonds.

The Forme of Cury, about 1390

CORMARYE

This recipe for a roast was not cooked on a spit as was common in medieval times, as it specifically tells us to 'lay it in the sauce, and keep that which falleth therefrom in the roasting'. It would have been cooked in a covered earthenware or iron pot placed in a brick oven, and a casserole or self-basting roasting tin will answer nicely.

SERVES 4

Piece of loin pork, about 2¼ lb
2 level teaspoons ground coriander
½ level teaspoon ground caraway seeds
1 level teaspoon salt

¼ level teaspoon ground black pepper
4 cloves garlic, crushed
½ pint red wine

Skin the pork and slash the fat with a knife. Put the coriander, caraway, salt, pepper, garlic and red wine into the roasting tin or casserole. Put in the pork, and cover with a lid. Roast in a moderate oven (350 deg. F or Gas No. 4) for 1½ hours. Start with the fat side up, turn after 30 minutes, and after 1 hour turn the meat again. Allow to finish cooking for a further 30 minutes with the lid off, to brown the fat.

Dish the meat and keep warm. Pour the juices from the roasting pan into a small saucepan and reduce to the consistency of gravy by boiling rapidly.

The Forme of Cury, about 1390

PEIONS YSTEWED

This dish provides an excellent opportunity of trying a truly medieval meal. The pigeons are served complete, one per person, on a plate or trencher of bread. They should be eaten with the fingers, so provide large finger bowls and plenty of napkins.

SERVES 4

4 pigeons
12 large cloves of garlic, whole
2 teaspoons chopped fresh thyme
2 teaspoons chopped fresh marjoram
2 teaspoons chopped fresh sage
2 tablespoons chopped fresh parsley

½ pint stock
3 tablespoons verjuice, or the juice of ½ lemon
pinch saffron
½ level teaspoon ground cinnamon
¼ level teaspoon ground ginger
½ oz lard

The pigeons should be plucked, drawn and ready for roasting. Remove any papery outer coating from the cloves of garlic. Dividing the garlic and herbs equally, stuff the inside of each pigeon with the mixture.

Place the pigeons in a casserole, choose one that is just big enough to take them. Pour over the stock, add the lemon juice, the saffron, cinnamon and ginger and finally the lard. Cover with a lid, place in the centre of a moderate oven (350 deg. F or Gas No. 4) and cook for 1½ hours or until very tender. It is especially important that the pigeons should be really tender if you are going to eat them by hand. They should be almost falling apart: if necessary allow an extra 15 minutes' cooking time to ensure this.

The Forme of Cury, about 1390

BURSEWS

These small pork rissoles are very filling and rich. Allow not more than 4–5 per person. Pounding the pork by hand is hard work; a mincer can be used, but take care not to blend the ingredients too finely – the texture should be that of a coarse pâté. Any cold left-over pork is ideal for this recipe.

SERVES 4

½ lb cold cooked pork
2 hard-boiled egg yolks
1 level teaspoon ground coriander
¼ level teaspoon ground nutmeg
1 level teaspoon salt
¼ level teaspoon pepper
¼ level teaspoon ground cinnamon

1 blade mace, crushed
2 whole cloves, crushed
½ level teaspoon caraway seeds, crushed
3 tablespoons flour
1 egg
1 oz dripping

Finely chop or mince the pork. Mash the hard-boiled egg yolks and add to the pork together with the coriander, nutmeg, salt, pepper, cinnamon, mace, cloves and caraway seeds. Pound or mash the mixture until it becomes a fairly smooth paste.

Shape heaped teaspoons of the mixture into small balls and roll each one first in flour and then in the lightly mixed egg to coat all over. From this mixture you should get about 20 rissoles.

Heat the fat in a fairly large frying-pan, add the pork rissoles and fry gently for about 5 minutes, turning frequently until they are brown on all sides.

The Forme of Cury, about 1390

EGURDOUCE

The old recipe is given for 'conyng' (rabbit) 'or kydde'. Although rabbit is more easily obtainable, it would make an excellent dish with kid. The meat is well browned and then topped with plumped raisins and lots of fried onion before simmering in spices and red wine. A recipe that turns a rather dull rabbit into a rich and aromatic stew.

SERVES 4

1 rabbit, or pieces of rabbit about 2 lb	*1 level teaspoon ground ginger*
2 oz lard	*1 level teaspoon ground cinnamon*
2 oz stoned raisins	*1 level teaspoon salt*
3 medium onions	*½ level teaspoon white pepper*
¾ pint red wine	

Wash and dry the pieces of rabbit. For a very tender dish soak the rabbit pieces overnight covered with cold salted water with a bay leaf, a blade of mace and a squeeze of lemon juice added. Drain and pat the pieces dry before using.

Heat the lard in a large frying-pan and add the rabbit pieces. Fry quickly, turning the pieces frequently until they are browned on all sides. Lift the pieces out and place in a large saucepan. Add the raisins to the hot fat remaining in the frying-pan. Fry for a few moments until they are soft and plump, then drain them from the pan with a slotted spoon and scatter over the rabbit pieces. Peel and chop the onions and add these to the hot fat. Add a little more lard if necessary and fry the onions until they are tender and beginning to brown. Drain with a slotted spoon and sprinkle over the rabbit pieces in the pan. Pour in the wine and add the ginger, cinnamon, salt and pepper. Cover and simmer gently for 1½ hours or until the rabbit is tender.

The Forme of Cury, about 1390

BEEF Y-STYWYD

The original recipe included cubebs. If you can obtain these from a specialist herb-grower, use ½ teaspoon of the powder and reduce the quantities of cinnamon, cloves and mace in the recipe by half. The cardamom seeds were called 'grayns of parise' and can be bought at most health shops and delicatessens. Original instructions suggest that the meat should be washed and the water strained to use as part of the liquid for the first stage of cooking. Unfortunately, or perhaps fortunately, meat from a modern butcher does not have the interesting accretions which would make this operation worthwhile!

SERVES 4

3½ lb fore-rib of beef, on the bone	*1 tablespoon chopped fresh parsley*
1 pint water	*1 teaspoon chopped fresh sage*
1 rounded teaspoon ground cinnamon	*2 level teaspoons salt*
2 whole cardamom seeds, peeled and crushed	*4 tablespoons fresh breadcrumbs*
(optional)	*1 tablespoon wine vinegar*
2 whole cloves	*large pinch saffron strands, soaked in*
5 blades mace	*2 tablespoons hot water*
2 large onions, finely chopped	

Cut the meat off the bone and trim away any excess fat. Dice the flesh and place in a saucepan. Add the water and the meat bone, which gives flavour to the broth. Bring to the boil, skim and allow to simmer for 30 minutes. Remove the bone. Add the cinnamon, cardamoms, cloves, mace, the finely chopped onions, chopped parsley, sage and the salt. Cover the pan and allow to simmer for a further 45 minutes.

Place the breadcrumbs in a bowl and add ⅓ pint (about 1 teacupful) of the hot broth taken from the pan of beef. Add the vinegar and strain the mixture into a second bowl. Leave to stand for 10 minutes.

Add the infused saffron to the beef and then the breadcrumb mixture. Taste and add more salt or vinegar as required. Allow to cook for a further 45 minutes – the stew should have about 2 hours cooking time in all.

Potage Dyvers, about 1420

SPYNOCHES YFRYED

This medieval way of cooking spinach is beautifully simple and subtle in flavour. After cooking, the spinach is turned in olive oil and enlivened with a little nutmeg. Butter, which we would add to spinach was seldom used for cooking in those days, but try the olive oil and you will find that it marries with spinach even more harmoniously.

SERVES 4
2 lb fresh spinach   little grated nutmeg
2 tablespoons olive oil

Wash the spinach and tear out the mid-rib. Add the leaves to a pan containing a small quantity of boiling water. Cover and cook for 10 minutes or until the spinach is quite tender. Drain the spinach well and press in a colander to remove all excess water.

Turn on to a board and roughly chop into squares with a knife. Return to a clean pan with the olive oil and a little grated nutmeg. Reheat gently, turning the spinach with a wooden spoon.

The Forme of Cury, about 1390

MAKKE

When one remembers that potatoes were unknown in medieval Europe, any floury or starchy vegetable made a good complement to other dishes. This purée of dried beans in winter, or broad beans in summer with the addition of a little wine, is nicer than mashed potato. The old recipe tells us to 'take oynons and mince hem smale seeth hem in oile til they be al bron and flourish the dissh therewith'. This is an appetizing and visual enhancement to the beans. 'Flourishing' a dish meant decorating it.

SERVES 4
8 oz dried butter beans (or in summer 1 pint   2 tablespoons oil
  shelled broad beans)   1–2 tablespoons red wine
2 large onions   salt to taste

Soak the beans overnight. Drain and put in a pan with plenty of cold salted water. Bring to the boil, cover and simmer for about 1 hour or until the beans are soft. Drain well and beat to a purée.

237

Peel and chop the onions finely. Add to the hot oil in a frying-pan and cook gently until the onions are tender and brown. Pour the warmed wine over the bean purée, stir and season to taste. Top with the browned onions and serve.

The Forme of Cury, about 1390

APPLE MUSE

There is a similar recipe in *The Forme of Cury* entitled Apple Moy which used ground rice instead of breadcrumbs to thicken a purée of apples. The word 'muse' used in this recipe will have a familiar ring to those who know the German term, *Apfelmus*, for apple sauce or purée. The additional flavours of honey, almond milk and saffron used here, give a subtle taste to this dish of apples.

SERVES 6

2 lb cooking apples
4 tablespoons water
¼ pint almond milk – see page 229
4 heaped tablespoons thick honey

2 oz fresh breadcrumbs
pinch of saffron
pinch of salt

Peel, core and slice the apples and place in a saucepan with the water. Cover and cook gently for 15–20 minutes or until quite tender. Draw off the heat and pass through a food mill or sieve to make a purée. Stir in the almond milk, the honey and the breadcrumbs, saffron and salt. Stir to blend and cook gently for a few minutes.

Serve hot or warm.

Potage Dyvers, about 1420

COMADORE

These little fingers of pastry filled with spiced apple, pears, tender figs and raisins stewed in red wine, are not unlike mince pies. The old recipe tells one to stir the mixture 'warliche', i.e. warily, 'to keep it wel from brenyng' and this is a wise instruction for it becomes thick and could stick to the pan. When cold, the mixture is cut into 'smale pecys of the greatnesse and the length of a litel fyner, closed fast in gode paste and fryed in oile'. They would make an original touch to a conventional Christmas dinner and could be kept warm or reheated in the oven. The filling can be made up in advance.

MAKES 26

¼ lb dried figs (if hard dried, soak
    overnight)
¼ lb stoned raisins
½ pint red wine
1 lb cooking apples
1 lb pears
4 oz castor sugar
2 tablespoons oil

3 cloves, crushed
3 blades of mace, crushed
½ level teaspoon cinnamon
generous pinch ground ginger
pinch salt
1 tablespoon flaked almonds
6 oz shortcrust pastry
oil for frying

Wash the figs and raisins and put them in a saucepan with the wine. Bring to the boil, then simmer for 30 minutes or until tender. Drain, reserving the liquor, and purée the fruit. Meanwhile peel and core the apples and pears and keep in cold water until needed.

Add the sugar to the reserved wine liquid. Stir over the heat until the sugar has dissolved and bring up to the boil. Strain on to the purée of fruit. Chop the apples and pears and place in the saucepan together with the fruit purée. Cook the mixture gently for 30 minutes, or until the fruit is quite soft.

Place the oil in a clean saucepan. Add the pulped fruit, the cloves, mace, cinnamon, ginger, salt and almonds. Cook gently, uncovered and stirring occasionally to prevent the mixture from sticking, until the mixture is really thick. Turn on to a flat dish, spread level and leave until quite cold.

On a floured surface roll the pastry out thinly to an oblong. Cut into pieces about 4 inches long and 2½ inches wide. Damp all edges and lay on each oblong of pastry a little of the filling the greatness, and length of a little finger. With floured fingers carefully seal the edges. Heat a little oil in a frying-pan and gently fry the comadores until golden brown, or place on an oiled baking tray, set in a moderate oven (350 deg. F or Gas No. 4) and bake for 30 minutes.

Serve on a hot plate dusted with extra sugar.

The Forme of Cury, about 1390

FOR TO MAKE TARTYS IN APPLIS

There are several descriptions of different types of pastry given in the medieval recipes and 'tartys' are generally referred to as 'fayre paste', which suggests that the pastry was eaten, as in the recipe, and not just used as a container. It is an example of dried fruits and apples being used to give a taste of freshness and variety to the winter diet, with spices and saffron to add an exotic flavour. Saffron was much used in the Middle Ages for flavouring and colouring. It was widely grown and therefore relatively less expensive than it is today.

SERVES 4–6

2 lb dessert apples	*1 pinch ground nutmeg*
1 lb pears	*2 tablespoons water*
2 oz stoned raisins	*pinch of saffron*
1 or 2 chopped dried figs	*4 oz short-crust pastry*
1 level teaspoon cinnamon	

Peel, core and cut up the apples and pears. Place in a good-sized saucepan along with the chopped raisins and figs, the cinnamon and nutmeg. Add the water. Cover the pan with a lid and cook very gently, shaking the pan occasionally, until the mixture is well pulped and reduced. Flavour with a pinch of saffron.

Line 8-inch flan ring with the short-crust pastry. Pour in the hot apple mixture and spread level.

Place above centre in a hot oven (400 deg. F or Gas No. 6) and bake for 35 or 40 minutes. Serve warm or cold.

The Forme of Cury, about 1390

FRUTOURS

These apple fritters are slim, tender and coated in the lightest of batters, achieved with the use of yeast and ale. The taste of the ale is just discernible. Follow the original instructions and having peeled and cored the apples 'cut hem thyn like obleies' (communion wafers). Four large cooking apples make a lot of fritters, but they melt in the mouth and will disappear fast.

SERVES 4
4 large cooking apples

FOR THE BATTER
4 oz plain flour	*½ level teaspoon sugar*
pinch salt	*6 tablespoons pale ale*
½ oz fresh yeast	*2 egg yolks*
3 tablespoons warm water	*2–3 oz butter for frying*

Sift the flour and salt into a bowl. Blend the yeast with the warm water and add the sugar. Pour into the centre of the flour. Add the pale ale, and using a wooden spoon draw in the flour and beat well to make a smooth batter. Cover with a cloth and leave in a warm place for 30 minutes. Lightly mix the egg yolks and stir into the batter before using.

Peel, core and slice the apples thinly. Dip them in the batter and then add to a frying-pan of melted, hot butter. Fry until they are golden brown, turning them to cook both sides. Fry a few at a time, adding flakes of butter to the pan as needed.

Serve the hot fritters dusted with castor sugar.

A Boke of Kokery, fifteenth century

RAPEYE

The old recipe is full of typical medieval ingredients and instructions. Dessert apples were used, and we are required to 'stampe hem' to achieve a pulped consistency. The dish was coloured 'wyth safran an wyth sauderys', the latter made from sandalwood and produced a rich red colour. A drop of cochineal is permissible if you want to make the dish resplendent, but the use of red wine helps the colouring as does the saffron. Finally the much esteemed almond milk is included and this should be made overnight, or a few hours before starting the recipe.

SERVES 4–6
4 oz dates	*2 blades mace, crushed*
½ pint almond milk, see page 229	*6 cloves, crushed*
2 lb dessert apples	*2 level tablespoons ground rice*
½ pint red wine	*pinch saffron strands, soaked in*
pinch ground ginger	*2 tablespoons hot water*
1 level teaspoon ground cinnamon	

Stone and finely chop the dates and put them in a saucepan with the almond milk. Peel, core and chop the apples and add along with the wine and the ginger, cinnamon, mace, and cloves. Bring to the boil, cover and simmer gently for 5 minutes. Mash apple with wooden or slotted spoon and continue to cook until soft and well pulped.

Stir in the ground rice and the infused saffron and cook for a further 20 minutes. Taste and add sugar if desired. The mixture should be fairly thick, or 'chargeaunt' as the old recipe describes the consistency. Serve hot with extra cinnamon sprinkled on top.

Potage Dyvers, about 1420

PEER IN CONFYT

This is a compote of pears first stewed in red wine, then simmered in a syrup of white wine, sugar and ginger. The old recipe tells us to use 'wyne greke' (Greek), but any sweet white wine would do. While the pears simmer in their syrup the kitchen is filled with the most heavenly warm, spicy smell. Serve cold, or hot with a jug of chilled thick cream if you agree to sacrifice absolute authenticity.

SERVES 4
2 lb cooking pears   *6 oz castor sugar*
½ pint red wine   *1 level teaspoon ground sugar*
½ pint sweet white wine

Peel, halve and core the pears. Place the pears cut side down close together in a shallow pan with the red wine. Bring to the boil, cover and stew gently for 30 minutes. Remove the pan lid for the last 10 minutes so that the wine is well reduced. Drain the pears.

Place the white wine, sugar and ginger in a clean saucepan and bring to the boil, stirring to dissolve the sugar. Simmer for 5 minutes, then add the pears and cook for a further 5 minutes. Serve in the syrup.

The Forme of Cury, about 1390

Recipes of the Seventeenth Century

ROGNONE DI VITELLA IN CROSTATE

KIDNEY PIE

Fresh buffalo milk cheese was used in the original recipe for this substantial kidney pie. I have substituted cream or curd cheese. Thinly sliced dry cured ham, such as Parma ham, may also have been used and, if you wish to be extravagant, it would no doubt enhance the flavour.

SERVES 4–6

12 lamb's kidneys	salt and pepper
6 tablespoons stock	4 slices cooked ham
3–4 oz cream cheese	8 oz shortcrust pastry
1 dessertspoon lemon juice	

Snip the core from each kidney, but leave the kidneys whole. Remove the skin and place the kidneys in a saucepan with the stock. Bring to the boil, cover and simmer for about 10 minutes until they are just cooked. Remove from the pan and reserve the stock. Dice the kidneys and place in a clean saucepan, adding 2 tablespoons of the reserved stock. Add the cream cheese and stir over a low heat until the cheese has melted. Add the lemon juice, season with salt and pepper and draw off the heat. Finely chop the ham.

Divide the pastry in two portions. Roll out one piece and use to line an 8–9-inch pie plate. Damp the pastry rim. Sprinkle the chopped ham over the base and pour the kidney mixture in to fill the pie. Roll out the remaining pastry and cover the pie. Trim and press edges well to seal. Place in a moderately hot oven (375 deg. F or Gas No. 5) and bake for 30–40 minutes, or until nicely browned. Serve hot.

Antonio Frugoli Lucchese:
Pratica e Scalcaria, 1631

ANATRE AROSTO

ROAST DUCK

The Italian recipe was cooked with wild duck, and when in season these should be used, with the combinations of fruits also in season. At other times the alternative combinations of fruit can be used with domestic duck.

SERVES 4

1 duck, about 3–4 lb	thinly pared rind of $\frac{1}{2}$ lemon
4 oz dried apricots, soaked overnight	1 peeled lemon
4 tablespoons apricot liquid – see recipe	

FOR SERVING

$\frac{3}{4}$ lb tagliatelli	lemon wedges

Prick the breast of the duck with a fork. Drain the soaked apricots and reserve the liquid. Stuff the duck with the apricots, the thinly pared rind of lemon and the sliced lemon flesh from which all pith and pips have been removed.

Place the duck in a roasting tin and add 4 tablespoons of the liquid in which the apricots were soaked. Place in a moderately hot oven (375 deg. F or Gas No. 5) and roast the duck, allowing 30 minutes per lb. When ready, the skin should be well crisped and brown.

Meanwhile add the tagliatelli to a saucepan of boiling salted water. Cook for 10–12 minutes or until tender, then drain well and keep hot.

Lift the duck on to a serving dish. Pour a few tablespoons of the pan juices over the tagliatelli and turn well to mix both together. Serve the tagliatelli beside the duck with the apricot stuffing spooned out and arranged on the tagliatelli. Add a garnish of lemon wedges. *Note:* The duck stuffing was given as 'various fruits' with sliced lemon. Dried apricots and lemons are good in winter. Green gooseberries with orange for spring. Cherries and red currants for summer. Well-spiced apples, perhaps with walnuts, for autumn.

Antonio Frugoli Lucchese:
Pratica e Scalcaria, 1631

LINGUA DI VITELLA

TONGUE

The mingled flavour of Seville orange and various fruits and vegetables in this early Italian dish of tongue is very unusual. If Seville orange is unobtainable, a mixture of sweet orange and lemon juice is very good. The cooking time is slow and long, but the result is melting, tender and fragrant.

SERVES 8

8 lambs' tongues	3 cloves
bouquet garni	½ level teaspoon ground cinnamon
4–6 peppercorns	salt and freshly milled black pepper
2 oz dried figs, soaked overnight	juice of 1 Seville orange or juice of ½ sweet
2 oz dried apricots, soaked overnight	orange and ½ lemon
3 rashers streaky bacon	2–3 pieces thinly pared orange rind
6 tablespoons stock	4 artichoke hearts
6 tablespoons dry white wine	¼ pint shelled peas

Put the tongues in a large saucepan with plenty of fresh cold water to cover. Add the bouquet garni and peppercorns and bring to the boil. Skim, then cover and cook gently for 1½ hours, or until tender. Test by piercing the tongue with a sharp knife blade at the tip. Lift the tongues from the pan and plunge into cold water. Peel away the skin and remove the bone and gristle at the root of each one.

Place the drained soaked figs and apricots in the bottom of a smaller pan or fireproof casserole. Add the trimmed bacon rashers cut in half, the stock, wine, cloves, cinnamon, a seasoning of salt and pepper, the strained orange juice and a few shreds of orange rind. Place the tongues on top. Cover the pan tightly and bring slowly to the boil. Simmer for 10 minutes, then transfer the pan to a slow oven (300 deg. F or Gas No. 2) and cook for one hour. Add the artichoke hearts and peas and cook for a further 20–30 minutes.

Serve the tongue on the bed of vegetables and fruits with juices from the pan poured over.

Antonio Frugoli Lucchese:
Pratica e Scalcaria, 1631

CHICKEN

The sauce for the chicken in this recipe is of such excellence that it is hard to believe how long ago it was invented. It is very easy and quick to make, yet its piquant delicacy lifts a roast chicken into the realms of *haute cuisine*.

SERVES 4–6
1 chicken, about 3 lb dressed weight
1 oz butter

½ pint chicken stock, made from the giblets

FOR THE SAUCE
2 egg yolks
½ pint beef stock
2 oz butter
1 tablespoon chopped fresh parsley

1 level teaspoon chopped thyme
¼ level teaspoon chopped tarragon
1 tablespoon wine vinegar
salt and pepper

French roast the chicken by rubbing the butter over the bird, cover the breast with foil and set in a roasting tin with the chicken stock. Place in a hot oven (400 deg. F or Gas No. 6) and roast for 1¼ hours.

About 10 minutes before the end of the roasting time for the chicken, prepare the sauce. Lightly beat the egg yolks in a small bowl and stir in the beef stock. Pour into a small pan and set over low heat. Add the butter in small pieces and stir constantly while the mixture thickens. Draw off the heat, stir in the chopped herbs and the vinegar slowly. Return to a low heat, season with salt and pepper and stir briskly until the sauce is nearly boiling. Then draw off the heat.

Take up the roast chicken, carve and arrange the pieces on a hot dish. Pour over the sauce and serve.

Max Rumpolt: *Ein neu Kochbuch*, 1604

NIMB LINSE . . .

LENTILS

If you can buy the brown or green lentils, they are very much nicer than the slightly bitter yellow ones. With the chopped bacon they make a good supper dish for a cold night, or a weekend lunch at home with bread and cheese. They keep hot and reheat easily.

SERVES 4
8 oz dried lentils, soaked overnight
1 pint beef stock
1 large onion
2 cloves garlic
½ level teaspoon salt
freshly milled black pepper

4 oz boiled bacon or ham
2 tablespoons chopped fresh parsley
pinch chopped marjoram
pinch chopped tarragon
½ teaspoon chopped chervil

Drain the soaked lentils, rinse well and place in a large saucepan. Add the beef stock and bring to the boil. Peel and chop the onion, crush the garlic and add both to the lentils with the salt and a seasoning of pepper. Cover and cook gently for about 1 hour, or until the lentils are quite soft. Drain and reserve about 3 tablespoons of the liquid from the pan.

Cut the bacon into small dice and put in a clean saucepan with the cooked lentils, chopped herbs and the reserved liquid. Stir and cook for a few minutes to thoroughly heat through. Serve hot.

Max Rumpolt: *Ein neu Kochbuch,* 1604

BÖHMISCH BABA

PEAS

The combination of smooth green pea purée with bacon fat, on a base of lightly fried bread is a delicious mingling of tastes and textures.

SERVES 4

12 oz shelled fresh peas or 4 oz dried peas,
*   soaked overnight and 8 oz frozen peas*
salt
4 oz butter

1 egg yolk
3–4 thin slices of stale white bread
½ oz bacon dripping

Cook the fresh peas in boiling salted water for 15–20 minutes or until tender enough to make a purée. Or, drain the soaked peas and cook in boiling salted water for about 20 minutes until soft, add the frozen peas, reboil and cook for a further 5 minutes. Drain the peas, reserving the liquid and put through a sieve or food mill. Add sufficient of the liquid to make about ½ pint soft purée.

Melt half the butter and stir into the purée with the lightly beaten egg yolk. Fry the bread slices in the remaining butter and use to line a round earthenware dish. Pour over the purée of peas. Melt the bacon dripping in a small saucepan and run the dripping over the purée. Set in a moderate oven (350 deg. F or Gas No. 4) and bake for 15 minutes. Serve hot.

Max Rumpolt: *Ein neu Kochbuch,* 1604

SPENAT TURTEN

SPINACH TART

The addition of Parmesan and mace give a special flavour to this spinach tart. It is taken from Max Rumpolt's book which is accepted as the first outside Renaissance Italy to include the more refined way of cooking out of which the classic French cuisine developed.

SERVES 4

1 lb spinach
2 oz fresh white breadcrumbs
2 rounded dessertspoons grated Parmesan cheese
¼ level teaspoon ground mace
¼ level teaspoon ground pepper

salt
2 egg yolks
2 oz butter
4–6 oz shortcrust pastry

Pull away the stems and soak the spinach leaves in plenty of cold water. Drain and cook, with no additional water, for about 10 minutes, or until just tender. Drain well, and chop roughly. Place the chopped spinach in a bowl, add the breadcrumbs, Parmesan cheese, mace, pepper and a pinch of salt. Mix well together. Lightly beat the egg yolks and stir into the spinach mixture. Melt the butter in a small pan and pour half of it into the spinach. Stir to mix the ingredients.

Roll out the pastry on a floured surface and use to line an 8-inch pie plate. Fill with the spinach mixture and pour over the rest of the melted butter. Set in a moderate oven (350 deg. F or Gas No. 4) and bake for 30 minutes or until the pastry is done. Serve hot.

Max Rumpolt: *Ein neu Kochbuch*, 1604

NIMB GERIEBENE MANDELN . . .

ALMOND AND RAISIN PUDDING

These little pastries have a sweet filling of almonds and raisins gently scented with rose-water. They are typical of the medieval puddings, made with dried fruits such as figs, dates and raisins. Presumably when fresh fruits were in season they found little need to make up such cooked desserts.

SERVES 4

2 oz ground almonds	*2 teaspoons rose-water*
4 oz raisins or currants	*6 oz shortcrust pastry*
2 oz castor sugar	*1 oz butter*

Mix the ground almonds, raisins and sugar in a bowl and stir in the rose-water. Using the hands, mould the mixture into a long 'rope' and cut into 16 small pieces. Shape each one into a little roll.

Roll out the pastry on a floured surface and cut into rounds the size of a small saucer, or into rectangles. Place a portion of the almond mixture on to each piece of pastry. Damp edges and fold over to enclose the filling. Seal the edges neatly.

Melt the butter in a shallow baking tray so that it is well greased and place the pastries on the baking tin. Set in a moderate oven (350 deg. F or Gas No. 4) and bake for 20 minutes. Sprinkle with castor sugar and serve hot.

Max Rumpolt: *Ein neu Kochbuch*, 1604

PASTICECCETTI DI DIVERSE CONSERVE DI FRUTTI

FRUIT PIE

The original recipe gave the filling as green gooseberries and red apples, with a conserve of mixed fruits with raisins, almonds or walnuts and spices as an alternative. Candied or crystallized fruits soaked overnight in a little wine to plump and soften them are nice as a filling, with some of the wine liquid reserved and added.

SERVES 4

8 oz plain flour
2 oz lard
2 oz grated marrow fat

2 oz sifted icing sugar
2 egg yolks
2 tablespoons water

FOR FILLING
4 cooking apples
½ teaspoon cinnamon

1 tablespoon castor sugar

FOR THE GLAZE
1 egg white

castor sugar to dredge

Sift the flour into a mixing basin. Add the lard cut into pieces with the grated marrow fat, and rub into the flour. Add the icing sugar, mix and make a well in the centre. Break the egg yolks into it, mix with a fork, adding enough water to make a firm dough. Roll into a ball and keep for an hour in a cold place.

Divide the pastry into two pieces, one a little larger, for the top. Roll out the smaller piece to line a buttered 8-inch pie plate. Spread with a layer of apple slices, sprinkle with cinnamon and sugar, then add another layer of apple. Roll out the remaining pastry for pie top, damp edges of pastry and seal. Cut 2 or 3 slits in top. Bake in the middle of a moderately hot oven (375 deg. F or Gas No. 5) or until the pastry is cooked.

Meanwhile make the glaze by lightly beating the egg white. When the pastry is cooked, remove from the oven, brush on the egg white and dredge with castor sugar. Return to the oven for a few minutes to brown the top.

Antonio Frugoli Lucchese:
Pratica e Scalcaria, 1631

Recipes of the Eighteenth and Nineteenth Centuries

SIMPLE SOUP

The author of this book wrote recipes for the family and for the sickroom. This particular recipe claims that the soup 'cannot be said to contain either gout or scurvy'. Whatever its medicinal properties, it has a fresh light flavour and is thick and satisfying. An excellent soup for the first taste of spring.

SERVES 6

2 large carrots
3 medium white turnips
3 medium potatoes
4 pints light stock
4 sticks celery
outer leaves of an average lettuce,
    excluding the heart

5–6 oz curly endive
1 oz parsley
salt and pepper
2 oz butter
1 oz flour

Peel and coarsely chop the carrots, turnips and potatoes and put them in a large saucepan with the stock. Wash and roughly chop the celery, lettuce, curly endive and parsley and add to the pan. Season with salt and pepper. Bring to the boil and simmer gently for 1–1½ hours, or until the vegetables are quite tender. Pass the vegetables and liquid from the pan through a sieve or food mill to make a purée.

Rinse out the saucepan and replace over the heat. Add the butter and when melted, stir in the flour. Cook for a few minutes, then stir in the purée and bring up to the boil. Simmer for 15 minutes. Check the seasoning and serve. The original recipes suggested that 'some part of the vegetables may be left unpulped' to provide some solid pieces in the soup, which is an alternative if you prefer.

Hunter's *Culina Famulatrix Medicinæ*, 1806

GREEN PEASE SOUP WITHOUT MEAT

This soup could be made with dried peas and frozen peas. For anyone with a garden, or even those faced with the end-of-the-season bullets sometimes sold in the shops, it is an ideal way of converting old peas into a delicious soup to which young peas, cucumber and lettuce give body and extra interest. The old recipe suggests that if not sufficiently green, some spoonfuls of spinach juice could be added.

SERVES 4–6

1 pint shelled old peas
2 pints water
2–3 sprigs mint
2 level teaspoons salt
½ pint shelled young peas
½ cucumber

1 medium onion
handful of lettuce, with as much stalk as
    possible
1 oz butter
½ level teaspoon ground pepper

Put the peas in a large saucepan with the water, mint and salt. Bring to the boil, cover and cook gently for about 40–45 minutes, or until the peas are soft. Remove the mint. Strain and reserve the liquor. Purée the peas through a food mill or sieve, adding a little of the hot liquor if the peas are very stiff to sieve. Return the purée to a clean saucepan and add the reserved liquor and the young peas.

Peel the cucumber and cut into cubes. Skin and chop the onion and wash and finely shred the lettuce and stalk. Add these to the pan of soup, along with the butter, pepper to taste and salt if required. Simmer for 25 minutes until the onion is tender, then serve.

Hunter's *Culina Famulatrix Medicinae*, 1806

TROUT

This is an original way of cooking trout. They are first stuffed with a soft herb and lemon-flavoured mixture, then cooked in wine and seasoning and finally served in their own rich, but delicate sauce. The old recipe used parsley and 'savoury herbs'. A little marjoram, dill, tarragon or chervil could replace the thyme and rosemary.

SERVES 4
4 trout

FOR THE STUFFING
4 oz fresh white breadcrumbs
1 oz butter
1 heaped tablespoon mixed chopped parsley,
  thyme and rosemary
1 level teaspoon salt

freshly milled black pepper
pinch grated nutmeg
grated rind of ½ lemon
1 egg yolk

FOR THE SAUCE
4 peppercorns
3 cloves
2 pieces finely pared lemon rind
1 onion
½ pint red wine

generous ¼ pint stock
4 tablespoons double cream
1 dessertspoon flour
1 tablespoon lemon juice

Ask your fishmonger to remove the heads and gut the trout without slitting the belly. If bought already cleaned, use cocktail sticks and thread to secure the fish closed after the stuffing. Wash and thoroughly dry the trout.

Put the breadcrumbs in a bowl with the softened butter, chopped herbs, salt, pepper, nutmeg, grated lemon rind and work all together with a fork. When evenly mixed, stir in the egg yolk. Divide the mixture into four portions and stuff the trout.

Lay the fish neatly in a large saucepan with the peppercorns, cloves, lemon rind, the onion thinly sliced and separated into rings, the wine and stock. Bring slowly to the boil. Cover and cook gently for 20 minutes. Lift the trout on to a hot dish and keep warm.

Mix the flour and cream together. Add the lemon juice and a little of the hot liquid from the pan. Stir to blend and return the mixture to the remaining pan liquid. Bring to the boil and stir until the sauce thickens. Pour the sauce over the fish and serve.

W. A. Henderson: *Housekeeper's Instructor or Universal Family Book*, about 1805

COD AND SHELLFISH

This anything but humble fish pie is typical of the lavish use of ingredients in the nine-teenth century. The spices and generous amount of butter would make a well-flavoured and rich pie with any fish, but the instructions are to take 'the same quantity of salmon' as cod, and 'when shrimps cannot be had, a tail of a lobster will supply their place'. When you are feeling extravagant, you will not be disappointed in this dish.

SERVES 4–6

1 lb cooked cod	*pinch of cayenne pepper*
1 lb cooked fresh salmon	*¼ level teaspoon black pepper*
or 1 large tin red salmon	*4 oz melted butter*
4 oz peeled fresh or frozen shrimps	*1 large egg*
¼ level teaspoon ground mace	*2 oz fresh white breadcrumbs*
¼ level teaspoon ground cloves	*a little extra butter*
1 level teaspoon salt	

Flake the cod and salmon into a basin and carefully remove any skin and bones. Roughly chop the shrimps, first draining off any liquid if using frozen shrimps, and add to the fish in the basin. Add the mace, cloves, salt and cayenne and black pepper. Melt the butter in a small pan and pour it over the ingredients in the basin. Lightly mix the egg and stir into the flaked fish mixture, add half the breadcrumbs and mix to bind the ingredients together.

    Butter an ovenproof dish, fill with the fish mixture and spread the top level. Scatter the remaining breadcrumbs over the top and dot with some flakes of butter. Set in a moderately hot oven (375 deg. F. or Gas No. 5) and bake for 30 minutes until well heated and the crumbs are crisp and brown.

Hunter's *Culina Famulatrix Medicinae*, 1806

TURBOT

The original recipe recommended using a whole turbot 'which in this mode of dressing must be small', but most recipes from the eighteenth century called for huge quantities, and even a small turbot would be large for most modern families and saucepans. Four nice thick steaks cut from across the fish make a good meal for four people and the beautifully rich and unusual sauce makes it worthy of a connoisseur. The use of two wines is extravagant, perhaps not essential, but decidedly delicious.

SERVES 4

4 steaks of turbot, about 1½ inches thick	*lard for frying*
flour	

FOR THE SAUCE

¼ pint dry white wine	*½ level teaspoon ground ginger*
¼ pint red wine	*1 oz butter*
3 anchovy fillets	*1 level tablespoon flour*
½ level teaspoon salt	*3 slices lemon*
little grated nutmeg	

Rinse the fish, dry very thoroughly in a cloth and then dip each piece both sides in flour. Select a pan large enough to hold the turbot steaks and set over moderate heat. Melt in it sufficient lard to give ½ inch of melted fat. When hot, gently place in the floured fish steaks and fry on both sides until golden brown and then lift from the pan and drain on absorbent paper.

Place the fish in a clean pan and add the wines, the anchovy fillets, salt, nutmeg and ginger. Cover and cook very gently for 25 minutes or until the liquid is reduced by half. Blend the butter with the flour and add to the pan liquid. Stir until the sauce thickens, then add the slices of lemon, cut free of pith and skin. Simmer for a further 5 minutes.

Lift the turbot on to a hot serving dish, the surfaces of which you have rubbed with a piece of shallot. Pour the sauce over the fish and serve.

W. A. Henderson: *Housekeeper's Instructor or Universal Family Cook*, about 1805

BEEF WITH CUCUMBER

You will get the best results with this dish if you have a really well-flavoured stock in which to cook the vegetables. A mixture of left-over brown gravy that was made with pan juices from a roast joint, plus an equal quantity of beef stock, made with stock or a bouillon cube, gives a good rich brown sauce. Serve at once to retain the delicate succulence of the cucumber.

SERVES 4
4 pieces of rump steak   *5 oz butter*
salt and pepper   *1 rounded tablespoon flour*
2 medium onions   *½ pint good stock*
2 cucumbers

Beat the steaks to flatten them and season with salt and pepper. Peel and thinly slice the onions. Peel the cucumbers, cut in four lengthwise and remove the seeds. Cut the cucumber flesh into 1-inch-long sticks.

Melt 3 oz of the butter in a large saucepan. Add the onions and fry gently until tender and brown. Add the cucumber, cover with a lid and cook gently for 5 minutes. Remove the pan lid and simmer for a further 10 minutes. Season well with salt and pepper and stir in the flour. Gradually add the stock, stirring all the time until the sauce has thickened. Cover and simmer for 10 minutes, or until the cucumber is quite tender.

Melt the remaining 2 oz of butter in a large frying-pan. Add the steaks and fry quickly on either side until well browned, then lower the heat and cook according to your own taste. Lift the steaks from the pan on to a hot dish. Pour over the cucumber and onion sauce and serve.

Hunter's *Culina Famulatrix Medicinae*, 1806

TO MAKE FRENCH CUTLETS, VERY GOOD

'Then butter as many pieces of white Paper as you have cutlets, and wrap them up every one by themselves, turn up the edges of the Papers with great care that none of the moisture

251

gets out; therefore let the Papers be large enough to turn up several times at the edge; and if occasion be, stick a pin to keep it all in; for this Gravy is all their Sauce.' This detailed description suggests that it was a new idea.

The use of paper was probably a natural development from the crusts of flour and water that were used earlier to protect all cuts of meat and poultry during cooking. Nowadays, foil is an easy substitute.

SERVES 8
8 lamb chump chops

FOR THE STUFFING

½ lb lean leg of pork, finely minced
½ lb fresh white breadcrumbs
½ lb shredded beef suet
4 anchovy fillets pounded with a small knob
  of butter
1 heaped teaspoon chopped thyme

2 heaped teaspoons chopped parsley
1 heaped teaspoon chopped marjoram
salt and pepper to taste
1 level teaspoon grated nutmeg
2 onions, finely chopped
3 egg yolks

Using a small sharp knife, trim the chops neatly and pull any skin away from the fat. Cut from the fatty side, through the meat towards the bone until each chop is almost halved horizontally.

Put all the ingredients for the stuffing into a large bowl, adding the egg yolks last. Stir to mix, and then knead well to bind the ingredients together. Take out small portions of stuffing and, without using flour, shape each portion into a roll the size of a small sausage. Flatten slightly and place one piece inside, and one on top of each chop.

Cut 8 pieces of foil 12 inches square and butter well. Wrap each chop individually, folding the foil edge tightly but allowing space for swelling. Arrange in a shallow roasting tin and place in a moderately hot oven (375 deg. F or Gas No. 5) for 30 minutes.

Unwrap the foil and serve the chops in their own juice.

By Several Hands: *A Collection of Above Three Hundred Receipts in Cookery, Physick and Surgery*, 1714

TO FRY BEEF STEAKS

The brown ale in this recipe gives a rich gravy and a fine flavour to the steaks, which should not be at all ragged as in a stew, but whole and tender.

SERVES 4

4 pieces rump steak, about 4 oz each
½ pint brown ale
1 large onion
2–3 sprigs thyme
small bunch fresh parsley

½ level teaspoon salt
freshly milled pepper
little grated nutmeg
½ oz butter
1 rounded dessertspoon flour

Trim and beat the steaks well with a rolling-pin to flatten. Put them in a large pan with the ale, bring to the boil slowly, then cover and cook for 10 minutes.

Slice the onion thinly. Wash and strip the herbs from their stalks and chop them finely.

Add the herbs and onion to the steaks with the salt, pepper and nutmeg. Work the butter and flour together, add to the pan and shake or stir to blend. Re-cover and cook gently for a further 45 minutes to 1 hour, or until the steaks are tender and the gravy thick and well flavoured.

Hannah Glasse: *The Art of Cooking made Plain and Easy*, 1760

TO FRICASSEY CHICKENS OR SWEETBREADS

It is important to follow the instructions of the original recipe which said 'set them on in as much water as will cover them; when they boil up scum them very clean, then take them out and strain the liquor'; this would be particularly important if using sweetbreads instead of chicken, but in either case it makes a great deal of difference to the delicacy of the final sauce, which has a beautiful texture and taste.

SERVES 6

4½–5 lb roasting chicken
water – see recipe
4 peppercorns
salt and freshly milled black pepper

1 blade mace
finely pared rind of ½ lemon
1 small onion, stuck with 4 cloves
¼ pint dry white wine

FOR THE SAUCE

1 level tablespoon plain flour
3 tablespoons cream
1 egg yolk

little grated nutmeg
juice of ½ lemon
½ oz butter

Joint the chicken, skin and wash the pieces and put in a large saucepan with enough cold water to cover. Bring to the boil and carefully skim the surface. Take out the chicken pieces, strain the liquid and reserve about ½ pint for further cooking.

Return the chicken pieces to the clean saucepan and add the reserved liquid. Add the whole peppercorns, a seasoning of salt and freshly milled black pepper, the blade of mace, pared lemon rind and the onion stuck with cloves. Cover with a lid and bring up to the boil. Warm the wine and add to the pan. Allow the chicken to simmer for 1½ hours, or until tender. Remove the pan from the heat and discard the onion.

Blend the flour, cream and egg yolk in a small bowl until smooth and add a little grated nutmeg. Add about 6–8 tablespoons of the hot chicken liquid and blend well. Gradually stir this mixture into the saucepan containing the chicken. Stir constantly as the sauce thickens and bring just to a simmer. Cook gently for 2–3 minutes, then add the lemon juice and butter. Stir to blend and serve.

By Several Hands: *A Collection of About Three Hundred Receipts in Cookery, Physick and Surgery*, 1714

HAUNCH OF VENISON

The Duke of Bolton's cook served venison in this way so that, though well done, it is exceptionally juicy and moist. The marinade in which the meat has lain is used to baste the joint during roasting. A caper sauce is served with the venison and is enriched with a 'cullis'. This was a special stock sometimes using quantities of veal, lean ham and chicken as well as vegetables, and was used solely to enrich sauces, stews or 'ragoos' as they were described. I give instructions for larding the joint which is part of the original recipe's excellence, but if you don't possess a larding needle, you may lay some rashers of fat bacon over the joint as it roasts.

SERVES 6–8
haunch of venison, weighing about 4 lb

FOR LARDING
2 rashers streaky bacon
1 level teaspoon salt
½ level teaspoon ground black pepper

½ level teaspoon crushed cloves
¼ level teaspoon grated nutmeg

FOR THE MARINADE
1 pint white wine
juice of 1 lemon
2 level teaspoons salt
2–3 parsley stalks
2–4 sprigs thyme

2–3 sage leaves
1 sprig rosemary
4 bay leaves
3 slices fresh lemon

FOR THE SAUCE
1 oz butter
the cullis — see recipe below
2 heaped tablespoons capers

juice of ½ lemon
pepper and salt to taste

Wipe the venison. Cut the bacon rashers into strips or 'lardons' ¼ inch wide and about 2 inches long. Mix the salt, pepper, cloves and nutmeg together and roll the 'lardons' in the seasoning. With a larding needle 'sew' each strip into the meat at intervals of about an inch.

Measure the wine, lemon juice and salt into a deep dish. Add the parsley stalks, thyme, sage, rosemary, bay leaves and lemon slices. Lay the larded venison in this and leave to marinate for 3–4 hours or overnight, turning the meat occasionally during the time.

Heat the butter in a self-basting roasting tin. Drain the venison from the marinade and place in the hot butter. Strain the marinade and add a few spoonfuls to the meat in the pan. Cover with the lid and set in a slow oven (325 deg. F or Gas No. 3) and roast for 2 hours. Baste with the rest of the marinade through the cooking time until it is all used up.

When the venison is tender and well cooked, dish and keep hot. Pour off the surplus fat from the pan. Put the 'cullis' and pan drippings that remain in a small saucepan and boil up. Continue to cook, uncovered, until the mixture is reduced to a strong gravy. Stir in the capers and lemon juice. Check seasoning and add pepper and salt if needed. Serve in a hot sauce-boat with the venison.

John Middleton (cook to the late Duke of Bolton, 1734): *500 New Receipts*

A FAMILY CULLIS

A simple version of 'a family cullis' can be made in advance, cooled and strained ready to use.

1 oz butter, rolled in flour
½ pint stock
2–3 oz mushrooms
3 tablespoons good gravy (left over from a joint or from brown jelly underneath the dripping)
1 glass white wine

bunch parsley, thyme and basil tied together
1 bay leaf
2 cloves
2 blades of mace
½ level teaspoon salt
¼ level teaspoon ground pepper

254

Melt the butter and flour in a saucepan. Add the stock slowly and stir to blend. Wash and slice the mushrooms and add them to the pan along with the gravy, wine, bunch of herbs, bay leaf, cloves, mace, salt and pepper. Bring to the boil, cover and cook gently for 1 hour. Cool, skim off the fat and strain through a fine strainer.

TO STEW A HARE

The long gentle cooking reduces the hare in this recipe to a very tender stew. The old recipe recommends 'stewing leisurely' for 6–7 hours, then to 'take out what bones you can find, with the herbs and onion, if not dissolved'. However, 2–3½ hours is quite enough cooking to tenderize the meat, if not to dissolve the herbs. The final instructions 'you need only shake it up with half a pound of butter when ready for the table' illustrates the lavishness of eighteenth-century cooking. A knob of butter is enough, but the claret recommended does greatly enhance the flavour of the gravy.

SERVES 4

2 lb hare pieces	½ level teaspoon ground black pepper
small bunch of parsley	1½ pints strong stock
2–3 sprigs thyme, marjoram and sage	1 pint claret
1 large onion	2 anchovy fillets
1½ level teaspoons salt	2 oz butter

Trim and wash the hare pieces. Dry thoroughly and put in a large saucepan with the fresh herbs tied in a bundle. Add the onion finely chopped, the salt and pepper and the stock. Bring slowly to the boil, cover and simmer for 1½ hours.

Add the claret and the anchovies pounded with 1 oz of the butter. Re-cover and cook gently for a further hour. Lift out the herbs and as many bones that are loose. Stir in the remaining butter and serve hot.

(By Several Hands) *A Collection of Above Three Hundred Receipts in Cookery, Physick and Surgery*, 1714

A WHIPT SILLIBUB, EXTRAORDINARY

The earliest syllabubs were made by milking a cow straight into a bowl containing some ale or cider. This was allowed to stand until a curd formed on the top of the ale-flavoured whey, which posed a practical problem, for the dish had to be partly eaten, partly drunk. Later on, wine was used in place of ale, and cream instead of milk. By the eighteenth century the proportion of cream was increased and the wine reduced until the final mixture was uniformly thick and of a delicious lightness and delicacy of flavour. It was then written of as 'an everlasting Syllabub'.

SERVES 6

thinly pared rind and juice of 1 lemon	2 oz castor sugar
scant ¼ pint white wine	generous ½ pint cream

255

Soak the pared lemon rind in the wine for 2–3 hours before starting the recipe.

Squeeze the lemon and strain the wine and lemon juice into a deep bowl. Add the sugar and stir well until dissolved. Slowly stir in the cream, then whisk with a hand or rotary whisk until the mixture thickens to a soft peak.

Spoon into glasses and stand in a cool place until next day. Choose a cool larder in preference to a refrigerator. This syllabub will keep 2 or 3 days.

By Several Hands: *A Collection of Above Three Hundred Receipts in Cookery, Physick and Surgery*, 1714

PANCAKES, CALL'D A QUIRE OF PAPER

These pancakes are the nearest in truth to the old 'melt in the mouth' description that I have ever come across. They are so rich, but thin and melting that their exquisite originality entirely justifies the wild extravagance of the ingredients.

SERVES 4

4 oz butter	*1 tablespoon sherry*
½ pint double cream	*1 teaspoon orange flower-water*
3 eggs	*1 rounded dessertspoon castor sugar*
2 rounded tablespoons flour	*little grated nutmeg, optional*

Melt the butter in a small pan, draw off the heat and allow to cool. Put the cream in a large mixing basin. Break in the eggs and mix together with a fork. Sift the flour and add to the cream and egg mixture, beating well to make a smooth batter. Stir in the sherry, the orange flower-water and the sugar and last of all the melted butter. Add a little nutmeg if liked.

Heat a small frying-pan and grease it with butter for the first pancake only. Pour in just enough batter to cover the pan very thinly and tilt the pan to spread the batter over the base. Cook one side, then flip the pancake over with a fish-slice or palette knife and fry the other side until speckly brown. Slide on to a hot plate and dust with castor sugar. Stack the pancakes, sprinkling each one with sugar until they are all cooked. Serve hot.

Hannah Glasse: *The Art of Cookery made Plain and Easy.* 1760

TO STEW GOLDEN PIPPINS A VERY GOOD WAY

Any yellow dessert apple can be used that will cook tender and clear-looking and hold its shape. 'Double-refin'd Sugar' was used in this and many of the eighteenth-century recipes. The sugar bought would have been coarse and dirty and would have needed further grinding and sifting.

SERVES 4

1 pint water	*juice of ½ lemon*
½ lb castor sugar	*2–3 pieces finely pared lemon rind*
6 Golden Delicious dessert apples	

Measure the water and sugar into a saucepan. Set over low heat and allow the sugar to dissolve. Bring to the boil and cook briskly for about 10 minutes.

Meanwhile thinly peel and core the apples. Drop them into a bowl of cold salted water to keep them white until all are ready. Rinse the apples and add to the hot syrup. Cook fairly fast for 8 minutes, turning once after 4 minutes, so that the apples cook evenly and become rather transparent in appearance.

Add the lemon juice and pared lemon rind. Simmer for a further 3 minutes, then draw off the heat and leave the apples until quite cold. Serve the apples in their syrup.

By Several Hands: A Collection of Above Three Hundred Receipts in Cookery, Physick and Surgery, 1714

THE BEST ORANGE PUDDING THAT EVER WAS TASTED

The rather fulsome title is hardly an exaggeration, this really is a mouth-watering sweet. The pastry case is filled with a luscious orange-flavoured amber jelly, rather like orange curd. The original used Seville oranges and the bitter-sweet taste is very subtle. But the grated rind of a lemon and a large sweet orange should be nice enough when Seville oranges are out of season.

SERVES 4
4–6 oz shortcrust pastry

FOR THE FILLING
4 oz butter
4 oz castor sugar
6 egg yolks

grated rind of 2 Seville oranges or the grated rind of 1 lemon and 1 large orange

Roll out the pastry and use to line an 8-inch buttered pie plate. Line with a square of greaseproof paper filled with a layer of rice, or with a piece of crumpled kitchen foil, to hold down the base of the pastry. Set in a moderate oven (350 deg. F or Gas No. 4) and bake 'blind' for 20 minutes. Remove the piece of greaseproof paper and rice, or foil, a few minutes before the end of the baking time.

Cream the butter, sugar and grated orange rind together. Beat in the egg yolks one at a time. When the mixture is smooth and creamy pour into the pastry shell. Set in a slow oven (300 deg. F or Gas No. 2) and bake for 45 minutes, or until the mixture is set and the top golden. If the top becomes brown a little too quickly, cover with a piece of foil after the first 20 minutes. Serve hot or cold.

A Collection of Above 300 Receipts in Cookery.
1714

FRENCH APPLE PUDDING

The original recipe observes, 'this dish differs very little from the English apple pie, when custard has been put to it. Custard and apple pie is the Shibboleth by which an Alderman may be known.' You don't have to be an alderman to enjoy this good pudding. It has interesting links with some medieval recipes through the combination of apples and almonds, but it is not at all like apple pie.

SERVES 4

2 lb dessert apples	3–4 bitter almonds (optional)
sugar to taste – see recipe	¼ pint cream
3–4 tablespoons water	1 egg
4 oz blanched almonds	1 level dessertspoon castor sugar

Peel, core and slice the apples. Put them in a saucepan with the sugar to taste and sufficient water to prevent them from sticking. Cover and simmer gently for about 10–15 minutes, or until the apple slices are quite tender.

Put the blanched sweet and the bitter almonds through an electric grinder. Turn into a bowl and stir in the cream. Separate the egg and stir the yolk into the almond mixture. Lightly whisk the egg white and fold into the mixture along with the level dessertspoon of castor sugar.

Spoon the cooked apples into an ovenproof dish. Pour the almond mixture over the apples and spread evenly. Set in a slow oven (300 deg. F or Gas No. 2) and bake for 30 minutes.

Serve hot with cream.

Hunter's *Culina Famulatrix Medicinae*, 1806

VICTORIA, APRICOT, PEACH or NECTARINE PUDDING

This is a very delectable sweet. The nineteenth-century cook says it may also be 'an iced pudding', but I think the breadcrumbs demand it to be eaten while still warm. Many dishes of this time were served in 'a paste border' or with borders of fried bread or toast cut into tiny triangles and fixed with egg white round the edges of the serving dish. This is one that recommends a paste border; a strip of pastry, the same depth as the filling, may be laid round as a wall before the pudding mixture is poured in.

SERVES 4

2 oz fresh white breadcrumbs	1 rounded tablespoon castor sugar
½ pint double cream	4 whole peaches, or 8 large apricots, or
2 egg yolks	12 Victoria plums
1 tablespoon white wine	1 egg white

Put the breadcrumbs in a bowl. Heat the cream in a saucepan until almost boiling. Pour over the crumbs and stir to blend. Cover the bowl and leave until cool. Then stir in the egg yolks, wine and sugar.

Poach the fruit in a little water until barely tender, then drain. When cool enough to handle, skin the fruit and remove the stones. Press the flesh through a coarse sieve or food mill to make a purée. Stir the purée into the blend of cream and breadcrumbs. Whisk the egg white until stiff and fold into the mixture. Pour into a shallow overproof dish. Set in a moderate oven (350 deg. F or Gas No. 4) and bake for 40 minutes. Serve hot with a bowl of lightly whipped cream.

Johnstone: *Cook and Housewife's Manual*, nineteenth century

Persian and Indian Recipes

Many of El Baghdadi's meat recipes begin with the intriguing instructions to 'melt fresh tail' or 'dissolve the tail' and throw away the sediment. The resulting oil is used for frying the meat. The Middle Eastern sheep are not docked as ours are to prevent much of the animal's fat going into the tail, thus the tail would have provided a plentiful supply of cooking fat. Instructions are given below for clarifying lamb dripping, which gives an absolutely clear oil for frying.

In the Indian recipes reference is constantly made to ghee and also to tyre. Ghee is very easy to make with clarified butter and will keep indefinitely. Tyre was made by adding a little buttermilk to warm fresh milk and letting it stand all night; in a hot climate the mixture would have soured by the morning, so we give a combination of sour cream and milk as a substitute. Finally, as well as most of the spices used in the Roman and Medieval recipes, turmeric is also needed and some dishes call for green ginger which can be bought from some health food shops and delicatessens, and from Chinese stores. It is the sliced root of fresh green ginger and is sold in small tins. As in the preceding recipes almonds and pine kernels are used and also pistachio nuts.

Here are the ingredients you may need to prepare yourself for some of the recipes.

SCENTED SYRUP

½ lb castor sugar
¼ pint water
juice of ½ lemon

1 dessertspoon rose-water
1 dessertspoon orange flower-water

Put the sugar, water and lemon juice into a saucepan. Bring to the boil, stirring until the sugar has dissolved and skim off the froth as it rises. Boil briskly without a lid for 10 minutes. Add both or one of the perfumed waters and boil together for 2 minutes more. Cool and chill. This syrup with keep indefinitedly in a bottle or screw-topped jar in the refrigerator.

SCENTED SUGAR

Store castor sugar in a screw-topped jar with a vanilla pod or piece of cinnamon stick, or both. (Camphor and musk were also used for scented sugars but these would seem rather strange to our tastes.)

GHEE

In a small saucepan melt $\frac{1}{4}$ lb butter (more, if you are going to store it). Heat gradually and skim off all the froth as it rises until the butter is as clear as oil.

TYRE

Take 4 tablespoons of sour cream and twice the amount of fresh milk. Mix together and use as directed in the recipes.

CLARIFIED LAMB DRIPPING

Simply heat the dripping saved from roast lamb gently in a pan. Pour through a strainer to remove the brown bits and use the remaining oil for frying.

SHIRAZ BI BUQAL

The old recipe describes this as 'an excellent relish which both awakens and stimulates the appetite'. It recommends dried curds or coagulated milk, for which we have substituted cottage cheese. The flavouring of chopped celery leaves, mint and leeks sharpened with mustard is deliciously original, and the topping of walnuts looks as good as it tastes.

SERVES 4–6

$\frac{1}{4}$ teaspoon chopped fresh mint

1 heaped tablespoon chopped leek (white part only)

1 heaped tablespoon chopped celery leaves

8 oz cottage cheese

pinch salt

pinch dry mustard powder

10 or 12 walnut halves, blanched to remove skins

Put the mint, leek and celery leaves through a parsley mill, or chop *very* finely. Stir into the cottage cheese with the salt and mustard.

Heap the mixture into a small earthenware dish and sprinkle over the coarsely chopped walnuts. Serve with bread or crispbread.

El Baghdadi, thirteenth century

MALIH BI KHALL WA-KHARDEL

The original medieval dish called for salted fish which being hard and dry would require long soaking. Smoked haddock makes an excellent modern substitute. The dish of plain rice absorbs the juices and it is delicious hot, but is also good cold if the haddock is flaked, mixed with a little rice and served with a salad.

SERVES 4

2–3 tablespoons sesame or nut oil

4 fillets smoked haddock, about $1\frac{1}{2}$–2 lb

4 tablespoons wine vinegar

$\frac{1}{4}$ level teaspoon dry mustard powder

1 level teaspoon ground coriander

pinch powdered saffron

Heat the oil in a frying-pan and fry the haddock fillets until lightly browned on both sides. Tip away surplus oil and pour over all but 1 tablespoon of the vinegar. Mix the remaining spoonful of vinegar with the mustard and add to the fish along with the coriander and saffron. Cover and cook gently for 10 minutes. Remove the lid and finish cooking for a further 5 minutes.

Serve the haddock on a bed of rice with all the juices poured over.

El Baghdadi, thirteenth century

LAHMA BI AJEEN

This is a traditional Arab dish. The result is small individual pizza-type savouries that are succulent and delicately spiced. When folded in half they are easy to eat in the fingers.

SERVES 4

6 oz plain flour
½ level teaspoon salt
scant ¼ pint water

pinch sugar
2 level teaspoons dried yeast
scant tablespoon sesame or nut oil

FOR THE TOPPING

1 large onion
1 tablespoon sesame or nut oil
½ lb minced beef
1 level teaspoon salt
¼ level teaspoon ground pepper

1 tablespoon chopped parsley or dill, or
   other fresh herbs
¼ level teaspoon ground allspice
1 rounded tablespoon ground almonds
½ level teaspoon sugar
1 tablespoon lemon juice

Sift the flour and salt into a warmed mixing basin. Heat the water until a little hotter than lukewarm – almost 110 deg. F or hand hot. Stir in the sugar and sprinkle in the dried yeast. Set aside in a warm place for about 10 minutes or until the yeast is frothy.

Pour the yeast liquid into the centre of the flour and add the sesame or nut oil. Stir with a wooden spoon to blend the ingredients, then mix by hand to a rough dough in the basin. Turn out on to a clean working surface and knead very well for about 5 minutes to get a smooth soft dough. Replace in the basin, cover and leave in a warm place until double in size.

Meanwhile prepare the meat topping. Finely chop the onion and fry gently in the hot oil to soften, but do not allow to brown. Place the minced beef in a mixing basin. Add the cooked onion, salt, pepper, herbs, allspice, ground almonds, sugar and lemon juice. Mix well by hand to get a smooth mixture.

Turn out the risen dough and press all over with the knuckles to knock out the air. Take small pieces of the dough, about the size of a walnut, and flatten with the heel of your hand to make circles about 4–5 inches in diameter.

Pile a generous quantity of the meat filling on each one and spread over the surface. Place on lightly oiled baking trays. Set in a very hot oven (450 deg. F or Gas No. 8) and bake for about 8 minutes. The dough should be just cooked, but still soft and unbrowned. Serve hot, each one is folded in half to eat.

Traditional Middle Eastern recipe

This may sound a complicated recipe, but it is not difficult if you get all the ingredients ready. There is plenty of time to make the meat balls and cook the eggs and rice while the chicken is roasting. It is a beautiful dish with plenty of subtle flavours and combinations, and the pan juices are wonderfully creamy and rich.

SERVES 6

1 roasting chicken, about 3½–4 lb dressed weight	*pinch powdered saffron*
1 lb boned shoulder or leg of lamb	*1 oz butter for roasting*
salt	*3 slices fresh green ginger*
1½ level teaspoons ground coriander	*½ level teaspoon ground cinnamon*
1 medium onion	*¼ level teaspoon ground black pepper*
½ level teaspoon ground ginger	*3 eggs*
4 cardamom seeds, peeled	*¼ lb clarified butter (ghee)*
4 whole cloves	*4 oz long grain rice*
4 tablespoons soured cream mixed with ¼ pint milk	

Wipe the chicken and set aside while preparing the stuffing. Cut up and mince about 6 oz of the lamb. Mix with a pinch of salt and 1 teaspoon of the coriander. Stuff this mixture inside the chicken. Peel and halve the onion and rub the cut onion surface over the chicken – reserve the onion for later in the recipe. Rub the surface of the chicken all over with the ground ginger. Crush 2 of the cardamom seeds and 2 of the cloves. Mix with the soured cream and milk, and the saffron to make a sauce for basting. Rub the butter for roasting around the inside of a roasting tin. Place the chicken in the tin and spread with a little of the basting sauce. Place in a hot oven (400 deg. F or Gas No. 6) and roast for 1½ hours, basting with the remaining sauce about 4 times throughout the cooking time.

Mince the rest of the lamb with 2 slices of the green ginger and place in a mixing basin. Add half the cinnamon and half the pepper, a good seasoning of salt and the remaining ½ teaspoon coriander. Stir in 1 egg white – taken from the 3 eggs, and mix by hand, squeezing the ingredients to a paste. Using wetted hands, shape spoonfuls of the mixture into about 12 small meat balls. Flatten each one a little and fry in about 2 tablespoons of the ghee until they are brown on all sides. Remove the meat balls from the pan and retain the pan drippings.

Finely slice the onion and the remaining green ginger. Mix in a bowl with the 2 whole eggs and the egg yolk. Add a little salt and pepper and mix well with a fork. If necessary add a little more ghee to the pan in which you fried the meat balls and when hot tip in the egg and onion mixture. Stir with a fork just as if making an omelette. Cook gently until the eggs have set firm, then draw off the heat.

Wash the rice thoroughly and drain well. Add to a pan of boiling salted water along with the remaining cloves, cardamom seeds and pepper. Boil for 10 minutes until the rice is barely tender, then drain well.

Return the rice to the saucepan and on top place the meat balls, and the egg and onion mixture, cut into pieces about 1 inch square. Run the rest of the ghee and 2 tablespoons of gravy taken from the roasting chicken over the contents of the saucepan. Cover with a tight-fitting lid, or foil and lid, to fit closely and cook gently for 10–15 minutes until the rice is quite tender and the meat balls and onion mixture heated through.

Spoon the contents of the pan on to a hot serving dish. Dish up the chicken separately and pour every scrap of the delicious juices from the tin over the bird.

Indian Domestic Economy, 1850

UNUNASS PULLOW

This is a very delicious sweet-sour dish. Half the flesh of a small fresh pineapple is cooked in a light sugar syrup for a final garnish to the meat; the other half is cooked, with spices added to the syrup, until it is brown and sticky, then combined with the meat to give a fresh chutney flavour.

SERVES 4

1½ lb boned shoulder or leg of lamb
1 large onion
¾ pint water
2 slices green ginger

1 level teaspoon salt
1 heaped teaspoon ground coriander
¼ lb clarified butter (ghee)
2 cloves

FOR THE PINEAPPLE AND SPICED SYRUP MIXTURE

2 oz castor sugar
½ pint water
juice of ½ lemon
1 small fresh pineapple
¼ level teaspoon ground cloves

½ level teaspoon cumin seeds
3 cardamom seeds, peeled and crushed
1 level teaspoon ground cinnamon
6 oz long grain rice

Trim and cut the meat into small, thick slices. Peel and slice the onion. Place the meat, onion, water, ginger – cut into narrow strips – salt, coriander and 1 tablespoon of the ghee into a saucepan. Bring to the boil, cover and simmer for 1 hour. When cooked, strain the gravy from the meat into a saucepan and set aside for cooking the rice. Heat 2 tablespoons of the remaining ghee in a large frying-pan with the cloves. Add the meat and onion mixture and allow to fry gently until the mixture begins to brown. Turn the meat pieces to fry on each side.

Meanwhile prepare the pineapple mixture. Dissolve the sugar in the water and lemon juice and bring to the boil. Pare the rind off the pineapple and cut the flesh into slices. Put half the pineapple slices into the syrup, cover and boil for 15 minutes. Remove the fruit and reserve for the garnish. Add the remaining pineapple slices to the syrup, this time with the ground cloves, cumin seeds, cardamom seeds and cinnamon added. Boil, with the lid off, until the syrup has nearly all evaporated and the mixture is sticky and brown.

Transfer the meat and onions from the frying-pan to the saucepan of spicy pineapple. Stir together and keep over a low heat. Bring the gravy that was reserved for cooking the rice, to the boil, add the washed rice and cook for 15 minutes. The gravy should all be absorbed by the rice.

Dish up the meat and spoon the cooked rice over. Pour over the rest of the ghee – about 1 tablespoon of the original quantity should remain. Garnish with the cooked pineapple slices and serve.

Indian Domestic Economy, 1850

MUJADDARA

This dish is subtly spiced with the earthy flavour of the lentils which, combined with the cinnamon, provides an interesting complement to the more positively spiced meat. It has no gravy with it, but the meat is so juicy that the dish is in no way dry.

SERVES 4

4 oz dried brown or yellow lentils, soaked
  overnight
2 lb boned shoulder or leg of lamb
2 tablespoons lamb dripping
2 level teaspoons ground coriander
2 level teaspoons salt

1 level teaspoon ground cumin
1 level teaspoon ground cinnamon
8 oz long grain rice
1 small piece stick cinnamon
water, see recipe

Drain the soaked lentils, then boil in fresh salted water for about 1½ hours, or until soft. Drain them well and reserve.

Cut the meat into cubes. Heat one tablespoon of the dripping in a heavy pan and add the meat. Fry to brown the pieces on all sides. Add the coriander and 1 teaspoon salt and pour in sufficient water to just cover the meat. Bring up to the boil and skim. Add the cumin and cinnamon, cover and allow to simmer for at least 1 hour. The meat should be very tender and the water absorbed or evaporated. If sufficient quantity of liquid remains, remove the pan lid and simmer a little longer until there is no excess liquid.

Heat the remaining dripping in a second saucepan. Add the cooked lentils and the washed rice, the remaining teaspoon salt and stick of cinnamon, crushed. Pour in about 1 pint water and bring up to the boil. Cover and simmer for 20 minutes until the rice is cooked and the water absorbed. Half-way through the cooking time check that the rice is neither sticking nor too dry and add more water if necessary.

Check the seasoning of the cooked rice and lentils, then put the cooked meat on top. Cover the pan with a cloth and a tightly fitting lid and leave over a very gentle heat, or draw to the side off the heat, for a further 30 minutes. It will not hurt to leave it longer.

El Baghdadi, thirteenth century

MUQARRASA

A bowl of rice is a suitable accompaniment to these savoury little meat cakes in their spicy juices. Being all meat they are quite filling and surprisingly do hold together in the pan without flour or egg to bind them.

SERVES 4

1 lb lean beef
3–4 cloves garlic
1 level teaspoon salt
½ level teaspoon ground black pepper
2 tablespoons lamb dripping

4 tablespoons warm water
1 rounded teaspoon ground coriander
1 level teaspoon ground cumin
1 level teaspoon ground cinnamon

Trim the meat and cut in pieces. Mince finely along with the garlic. Place in a basin and season with the salt and pepper. Beat and mix the ingredients well to bind together. Using wetted hands shape spoonfuls of the mixture into balls – you should get about 10 balls. Flatten each one into a round meat cake.

Heat the dripping in a frying-pan. Add the meat cakes and fry to brown on both sides. Pour away surplus fat and add the water. Simmer gently, uncovered, until the liquid has nearly all evaporated. Sprinkle with the coriander, cumin and cinnamon. Cover with a lid and leave over a very low heat for an hour, or until ready to serve.

El Baghdadi, thirteenth century

SHURBA

This is a very aromatic dish with a good distinctive flavour. The chick peas are delicious and unusual, and as the whole is cooked with well-spiced rice, it is a meal on its own. A dish of finely shredded cabbage cooked in a little wine, or vinegar and water, with a few caraway seeds, goes well with it.

SERVES 4

2 lb boned shoulder or leg of lamb
¼ lb lamb dripping
½ pint lukewarm water
2 oz chick peas, soaked overnight

piece cinnamon stick, about 2 inches long
1 level teaspoon salt
2 rounded teaspoons dried dill

FOR THE RICE

6 oz long grain rice
½ pint lukewarm water
¼ level teaspoon ground black pepper
1 level teaspoon ground ginger

3 level teaspoons ground coriander
1 level teaspoon ground cumin
1 level teaspoon ground cinnamon

Trim and cut the meat into small pieces. Heat the dripping in a large saucepan, add the meat and brown all over. Drain off the surplus fat and pour in the water – there should be just sufficient to cover the meat. Add the chick peas, cinnamon, salt and dill. Cover the pan and cook gently for 1½ hours or until the meat is tender.

Wash the rice and add to the pan of meat with the water, pepper, ginger and coriander. Bring up to the boil and cook gently until the rice is tender. Taste and add more salt if necessary. Sprinkle with the cumin and cinnamon and set over a very low heat until ready to serve. A simmering mat is very useful to prevent scorching and you may safely leave it for an hour.

El Baghdadi, thirteenth century

KULLEAH KOONDUM

This is an appetizing dish of fragrant curry-flavoured stew topped with hard-boiled eggs coated in a spicy meat jacket. If you want to serve a whole egg to each person, buy a ¼ lb more meat for mincing and increase the onion and spices a little. In any case you can vary the proportions of spice according to your taste, but always so they enhance, not smother, the flavour of the meat.

SERVES 4

1½ lb boned leg of lamb
1 lb onions
¼ level teaspoon ground cloves
¼ level teaspoon ground cinnamon
1 rounded teaspoon ground coriander
1 rounded teaspoon ground ginger

4 oz clarified butter (ghee)
¼ pint water
1 tablespoon flaked almonds
2 hard-boiled eggs
flour – see recipe
squeeze lemon juice or lime juice

Trim the meat and mince ¼ lb of the raw lamb finely. Chop 6 oz of the onions and mix the minced meat and onions together. Mix the cloves, cinnamon, coriander and ginger in a small basin. Heat a little of the ghee in a frying-pan. Tip in the minced meat and onion mixture and add 1 rounded teaspoon of the spice mixture from the small basin. Stir all to-

265

gether until the onions are soft, but not browned. Turn into a basin and set aside. Reserve any juices in the pan.

Cube the rest of the meat and slice the remaining onions. Heat a little of the remaining ghee in a saucepan. Add the meat pieces, the sliced onions, the remaining spice mixture and any juices remaining in the frying-pan after cooking the minced meat and onion mixture. Stir over the heat until the ingredients are blended and beginning to brown. Add the water and bring to the boil. Cover and cook gently for 45 minutes. Add the flaked almonds and cook for a further 5 minutes.

Meanwhile pass the fried meat and onion mixture through a fine mincer twice. Then squeeze the mixture to a paste with the hand. Shell the hard-boiled eggs, prick them over with a fork. Divide the meat mixture equally and flatten out each piece on a floured surface. Wrap a portion round each egg. Roll the eggs lightly in flour and fry them carefully in the remaining ghee. Cut the eggs in half lengthways to allow half an egg per person.

Dish the curry stew with a squeeze of lemon or lime juice over it. Place the eggs on top and serve with a dish of rice.

Indian Domestic Economy, 1850

KUBAB FOWL OR MEAT

The chicken in this recipe is first rubbed with powdered spices, and then basted during its roasting time with a delicious cream and onion sauce, flavoured with turmeric. The mixture has a gentle curry flavour, far more subtle than any of the hot-tasting ready-made curry powders give. The original recipe suggests that a shoulder of mutton can also be prepared this way.

SERVES 4–6

1 roasting chicken, about 4 lb dressed weight	*3 cloves, crushed*
4 teaspoons ground coriander	*1 level teaspoon ground black pepper*
1 level teaspoon ground ginger	*1 level teaspoon salt*
2 cardamom seeds, peeled and crushed	*1 oz clarified butter (ghee), for roasting*

FOR THE BASTING MIXTURE

1 medium onion	*1 tablespoon currants*
2 oz clarified butter (ghee)	*2 rounded tablespoons double cream*
1 level teaspoon turmeric	*2 rounded tablespoons soured cream mixed*
1 tablespoon flaked almonds	*with 4 tablespoons milk*

Prick the chicken all over with a sharp knife. Mix together the coriander, ginger, crushed cardamom seeds, crushed cloves, pepper and salt. Rub this mixture all over the chicken. Set the chicken in a roasting tin containing the 1 oz ghee. Place in a moderately hot oven (375 deg. F or Gas No. 5) to roast.

Meanwhile prepare the basting sauce. Peel and slice the onion and fry in the ghee with the turmeric until the onion is soft but not brown. Stir in the almonds and currants. Add the fresh cream and the soured cream mixed with the milk. Stir the ingredients thoroughly together and draw off the heat.

When the chicken has been roasting for 20 minutes, baste with half the onion and cream mixture. After another 10 minutes, baste again with the rest of the mixture and lower the oven temperature if the chicken is browning too quickly. Baste again once or twice with the juices in the tin during the total cooking time of 1½ hours.

Serve on a hot dish with all the sauce from the roasting tin poured over the chicken.

Indian Domestic Economy, 1850

DOEPEAZA DILAEE KHANEE

The selected spices give a faint and subtle taste of curry without hotness, while the creamy sauce flavoured with onions and almonds adds a marvellous taste and texture. The small whole onions that the original recipe gives are a worthwhile addition to this fragrant stew.

SERVES 4

1 lb lean stewing steak
12 cloves
5 cardamom seeds
$\frac{1}{4}$ level teaspoon ground black pepper
1 level teaspoon ground cinnamon
1 heaped teaspoon ground turmeric
1 rounded tablespoon sour cream mixed with
   2 tablespoons milk
6 oz clarified butter (ghee)

$\frac{1}{2}$ pint warm water
1 large onion
pinch saffron strands soaked in 2 tablespoons
   hot water
6 small whole onions
salt – see recipe
2 oz ground almonds
1 tablespoon cream

Trim the meat and cut into thin slices. Crush the cloves and cardamom seeds and place in a basin with the pepper, cinnamon and turmeric. Stir in the soured cream mixed with the milk and blend well. Add the slices of meat and turn them in the mixture to coat well.

Heat a little more than half the ghee in a large saucepan. Add the pieces of meat and fry gently to brown on both sides. Pour the warm water into the bowl which contained the spice and sour cream mixture, stir well to blend in any remaining mixture and then pour over the meat in the saucepan. Cover with a lid and simmer gently over low heat for 1 hour.

Peel and thinly slice the large onion. Fry gently in the remaining ghee until tender and golden brown. Stir in the infused saffron and the water in which it soaked. Set aside.

Peel the small onions leaving them whole and prick them all over with a fork. Rub them well with salt – preferably ground salt crystals. Remove the lid from the pan of meat and add the whole onions. Allow to simmer gently, uncovered for a further 30 minutes or until the meat is tender.

Before serving, take out about $\frac{1}{4}$ pint of the cooking liquor from the meat and blend it with the ground almonds and the cream. Pour over the meat and add the fried onion and saffron mixture. Simmer gently together for 5–10 minutes.

Serve hot with rice as an accompaniment.

Indian Domestic Economy, 1850

SANBUSAJ and SANBUNIYA

Here are two recipes, the first savoury and the second sweet that can be made from the same dough. *Sanbusaj* are little triangles of pastry stuffed with minced beef, flavoured with spices, lemon and chopped walnuts. *Sanbuniya* should be even tinier triangles or half-circles of pastry stuffed with a sweet scented almond paste and while hot dipped in cold syrup and dusted with scented sugar. They are dainty and delicious morsels.

Both sweet and savoury recipes produce adequate triangles for 4 servings.

FOR THE PASTRY DOUGH
1 lb plain flour
4 oz butter
6 tablespoons sesame or nut oil

5 tablespoons warm water
pinch salt

Sift the flour. Place the butter and oil in a large mixing basin and set over a saucepan of hot water to allow the butter to melt. Stir in the water and the salt. Remove the basin from the heat and gradually stir in the sifted flour. The mixture will form a soft greasy ball. Do not handle too much.

Set aside in a cool place while preparing the fillings.

SAVOURY FILLING FOR SANBUSAJ
½ lb minced beef
5 tablespoons water
squeeze lemon juice
salt and milled black pepper
1 level teaspoon ground coriander

¼ level teaspoon ground cumin
pinch dried mint (more if fresh is available)
1 oz walnuts, skinned and chopped
1 small egg
oil for frying

Place the minced beef, water, lemon juice and a good seasoning of salt and pepper in a saucepan. Add the coriander, cumin and dried mint. Cover and simmer gently for about 15 minutes. Towards the end of the cooking time remove the lid and allow any excess liquid to evaporate. The meat should be moist, but not wet. Add the walnuts and stir well. Remove the pan from the heat and stir in the lightly beaten egg. Return to the heat and stir until the egg has thickened. Allow the mixture to cool.

Take half the quantity of pastry dough and roll out very thinly on a floured surface. Cut into 3-inch squares. Place a spoonful of the filling on each and fold into triangles. Trim and pinch the edges together.

Either place on an oiled baking tray, set in a moderate oven (350 deg. F or Gas No. 4) and bake for 30 minutes. Or, fry gently in hot oil until golden on each side. Drain on absorbent paper. Eat hot or cold.

MUKALLAL FILLING FOR SANBUNIYA
2 oz ground almonds
2 oz castor sugar
4 teaspoons rose-water

oil for frying
scented syrup – see page 259
scented sugar – see page 259

Put the ground almonds, sugar and rose-water into a bowl and stir them together.

Take half the quantity of pastry dough and roll out very thinly on a floured surface. Cut in small squares of about 2 inches, or stamp out circles with a rounded pastry cutter. Put teaspoons of the filling into the centre of each. Fold over into tiny half-triangles or half-circles and seal the edges together carefully.

Either place on an oiled baking tray, set in a moderate oven (350 deg. F or Gas No. 4) and bake for 30 minutes. Or, fry in hot oil until golden brown. Drain on absorbent paper. Dip while still hot into scented syrup and dust with scented sugar. Eat cold.

El Baghdadi, thirteenth century

BASBOUSA BIL LOZ

Here is a delicate little sweet, tasting of almonds and lemon. Pour into small china or earthenware pots and serve cool or warm, but not chilled. A few toasted almonds, or a spoonful of whipped cream, or both, make an attractive topping to each pot.

SERVES 4

6 oz castor sugar
¾ pint water
juice of 1 lemon

3 oz butter
2 oz blanched and chopped almonds
2 oz semolina

Heat the sugar, water and lemon juice in a pan. Stir until the sugar is dissolved, then boil for 3 minutes.

Melt the butter in a second saucepan, add the almonds and semolina. Stir together and fry gently until golden. Stir in the syrup slowly and cook over gentle heat until the mixture thickens – this takes about 5 minutes. Remove from the heat and allow to cool for a few moments, stirring occasionally to prevent a skin forming. Pour into small individual pots and serve.

Early Middle Eastern recipe

AQRAS MUKALLALA

These small soft white loaves are filled with a sweet pistachio paste, or alternatively an almond paste. As soon as they come from the oven they are dipped in cold scented syrup and rolled in scented sugar. This does not leave them heavily sticky, the hot bread only absorbs a thin sheen of syrup. When sliced diagonally, the line of green pistachio filling shows prettily in each slice. Make the scented syrup in advance so that it is thoroughly chilled.

MAKES 4 SMALL LOAVES

½ lb plain flour
1 level teaspoon salt
¼ pint mixed milk and water in equal parts
1 level teaspoon sugar
2 level teaspoons dried yeast

1 tablespoon sesame or nut oil
pistachio paste – see recipe
scented syrup – see page 259
scented sugar – see page 259

Sift the flour and salt into a warmed mixing basin. Heat the mixed milk and water to a little hotter than lukewarm – about 110 deg. F or hand-hot. Stir in the sugar and sprinkle in the dried yeast. Set aside in a warm place for about 10 minutes or until the yeast is frothy.

Pour the yeast liquid into the centre of the flour and add the sesame or nut oil. Stir with a wooden spoon to blend the ingredients, then mix by hand to a rough dough in the basin. Turn out and knead very well for about 5 minutes to get a smooth, soft dough. Replace in the basin, cover and leave in a warm place until double in size.

Prepare the pistachio or almond paste according to the recipes given below.

Turn the risen dough out, press all over with the knuckles to knock out the air and divide the dough into 4 pieces. Roll each piece out to a 'rope' of about 6 inches, and flatten with the hand. Roll a portion of the pistachio paste to a thinner rope of the same length and place one down the centre of each portion of dough. Fold the dough over and pinch the edges together to seal. Place the loaves on an oiled baking tray with the sealed edges underneath. Leave in a warm place to prove until puffy. Set in a very hot oven (450 deg. F or Gas No. 8) and bake for 20 minutes. Remove each one from the oven and dip immediately into the cold scented syrup. Roll in scented sugar and leave to cool.

PISTACHIO FILLING

2 oz pistachio nuts   *2 dessertspoons scented syrup – see page 259*
2 oz castor sugar

Blanch the nuts in boiling water, drain and remove the skins. Pass the nuts through a nut mill to grate finely. Mix the nuts, sugar and sufficient of the scented syrup together to make a stiff paste.

ALMOND FILLING, CALLED KHUSHKRANAJ

2 oz ground almonds   *4 teaspoons rose-water*
2 oz scented sugar – see page 259

Almond filling makes a delicious alternative to pistachio, though not so attractively coloured. Measure the ground almonds, sugar and rose-water into a basin. Mix the ingredients together to make a stiff paste.

El Baghdadi, thirteenth century

Chinese Recipes

PICKLED PRAWNS FROM MADAME WU'S COOK BOOK

Madame Wu's domestic handbook called the *Chungkuei Lu* is probably the earliest Chinese cook-book. It dates from the Sung Dynasty of the tenth to twelfth century A.D.

2 lb live prawns	1 tablespoon peppercorns
3 oz sea salt	¼ pint rice wine or dry sherry
1 oz table salt	

Trim the tails and feelers off the prawns, but do not wash. Sprinkle and rub thoroughly with the sea salt. Leave to season for 3 hours in a refrigerator. Turn the prawns into a colander, set in a deep dish to drain away the extracted water and then replace in the refrigerator for a further 3 hours. Crush the peppercorns in a mortar just before using.

Empty the prawns into a jar. Sprinkle with the table salt, crushed peppercorns and the wine. Turn the prawns over in the mixture a few times. Seal the jar and leave the contents to stand for 1 week at room temperature after which time the prawns should be delicious and ready to eat.

ROYAL CONCUBINE CHICKEN

The royal concubine referred to in this case is Empress Yang Kwei-fei of the Tang Dynasty, A.D. 618–905. She was a great beauty but also a drunkard. Hence the chicken dish named after her was a dish which could be called 'Inebriated chicken', as it had a high alcoholic content!

1 chicken, about 3 lb dressed weight	2 stalks spring onions
2 slices root ginger	oil for deep frying
1 medium onion	1¼ pints chicken stock
2 tablespoons soya sauce	3 level teaspoons salt
pepper to taste	1½ pints white wine

Chop the ginger and onion coarsely and place in a bowl. Add the soya sauce and pepper to taste. Stir to blend the ingredients and then rub the chicken inside and out with the mixture. Leave for 3–4 hours to season. Cut the spring onions into ½-inch segments.

Drain the chicken and deep fry in hot oil for 7–8 minutes. Immediately immerse the chicken in a large pan of boiling water to remove all the grease. Place the chicken in a casserole and pour in the stock. Add the ginger and onion mixture and the salt, sprinkling them over the chicken. Bring the contents of the casserole up to the boil over direct heat, then transfer to a moderately hot oven (375 deg. F or Gas No. 5) and cook for 45 minutes. Skim the surface of the liquid generously to remove all fat and impurities. Turn the bird over and replace the casserole in the oven to cook for a further 30 minutes. Skim again carefully removing all impurities that have risen to the surface. Add the wine and replace the casserole in the oven to cook for a final 45 minutes.

Serve in the casserole. The chicken should be very winey but pure in flavour and tender enough to take to pieces with a pair of chopsticks, symbolical of the qualities of the royal concubine and her tragic life. Although frequently drunk, her love for the Emperor was pure. In the end she was executed by the military leaders who demanded her life for having led the Emperor astray, during a rebellion which eventually spelled the doom of the once-powerful Tang Dynasty.

BEGGARS' CHICKEN

In early Chinese history, before 1500 B.C., as probably in other parts of the world, poultry and animals were cooked by burial in hot coal, charcoal or at the bottom of a bonfire. First they were thickly coated with mud. This was usually done without evisceration and the method of cooking was termed 'Mao Pao' or scorched hair parcel, probably referring to the fact that the animal or bird was cooked feather or fur included. The present recipe, which is still used in China, is included mainly because of its adherence to the old method, although these days the animal is eviscerated first.

3–4 lb freshly killed chicken	*4 tablespoons rice wine or dry sherry*
2 medium onions	*2 tablespoons water*
3 slices root ginger	*2 level teaspoons sugar*
3 tablespoons rice	*4–5 lb potter's clay*
2 tablespoons soya sauce	

Remove the head, feet and all the intestines of the chicken. Chop the onion, shred the ginger and mix in a basin with the rice, soya sauce, wine, water and sugar. Stuff the mixture into the body cavity of the chicken.

Dig a square hole of approximately 2 feet by 1½ feet deep in the ground. Build a big bonfire in the hole with ample firewood. Meanwhile cover the chicken with a thick layer of potter's clay. See that every part of the chicken is well covered, then wrap the covered chicken in a piece of newspaper and secure with string.

After the bonfire has been burning for 25–30 minutes, dig a hole in the centre of the fire and put in the wrapped chicken. Pile all the hot cinders, sand and soil and burning firewood on top. Leave the chicken to cook in the pit for at least 2 hours.

Dig the chicken out of the pit. Leave until the clay has cooled somewhat, then break the clay with a chopper and remove with the hands. The feathers and skin will come away and the chicken flesh will be well cooked and moist. It should be possible to remove it from the carcass with a pair of chopsticks. The stuffing should be delicious.

Note: During the Boxer Rebellion of 1900, the Empress Dowager had to escape from Peking, when the International Expeditionary Force was approaching the capital. During her hiding in Jehol she was given this chicken which she thoroughly enjoyed. On her return to the capital she ordered it to be included among her court dishes.

STIR-FRIED DICED CHICKEN CUBE WITH SHRIMPS

This is a far more civilized dish than any of the previous ones and is said to have dated from the time of Emperor Chien Lung's tour of the south in A.D. 1784 when he encountered and enjoyed many delicious dishes which he had not eaten before. In the northern city of Peking one seldom ate meats cooked with seafoods which was common practice in the south.

½ lb breast of chicken
¾ lb shelled shrimps
1½ level teaspoons salt
2 level teaspoons cornflour
1 slice root ginger
1 medium onion

2 tablespoons vegetable oil
1 tablespoon sesame oil
¼ lb green peas
2 tablespoons soya sauce
1½ level teaspoons sugar
2 tablespoons rice wine or dry sherry

Dice the chicken into ½-inch cubes. Sprinkle the chicken pieces and the shrimps with the salt and cornflour and rub well in. Shred the ginger and chop the onion coarsely.

Heat the oil in a large frying-pan. Add the onion and ginger and stir-fry over high heat for ¾ minute. Add the chicken and stir-fry quickly for ½ minute, then add the shrimps and continue to stir-fry for a further ½ minute. Add the sesame oil. Stir and scramble a few times. Add the peas, followed by the soya sauce, sugar and wine. Continue to stir and scramble for a further minute. Serve on a well-heated dish.

THE NOMAD'S BAKED LUNCH

This recipe is derived from the Yuan or Mongol Dynasty A.D. 1279–1356. The original recipe follows a method of cooking similar to the one employed in the Beggar's Chicken. A whole unskinned lamb with head, feet and innards removed would be wrapped in clay and cooked in a deep pit. This was probably a common method employed on the steppes of Mongolia before Mongolian habits became more civilized after they had settled in China. Something more suitable for a modern kitchen can be prepared from the following recipe which will yet retain much of the Mongolian flavour.

1 leg of lamb, about 5–6 lb
¾ lb lamb's kidney
1 lb lamb's liver
2 large onions
3 lb potatoes or yams
3 slices root ginger

6 tablespoons soya sauce
4 tablespoons rice wine or dry sherry
1½ tablespoons brown sugar
pepper to taste
4 tablespoons chopped parsley

Remove the bone from the leg of lamb with as few cuts of a sharp knife as possible. This leaves a cavity to be filled with the stuffing.

Trim and chop the kidney and liver. Peel and chop the onion and potato into ½-inch cubes. Place these in a large basin. Mince or finely chop the ginger and place in a second basin with the soya sauce, wine, sugar and pepper. Mix well and add half the mixture to the prepared meat and vegetables. Rub the leg of lamb thoroughly both inside and out, with the remainder of the mixture. Leave the lamb and the stuffing to marinade for 1 hour.

Press the stuffing ingredients into the cavity in the leg of lamb. Enclose them tightly by wrapping the stuffed joint in two layers of kitchen foil. Set in a roasting tin.

Preheat the oven to very hot (450 deg. F or Gas No. 8) and place the lamb in the centre and bake for 45 minutes. Reduce the oven heat to 400 deg. F or Gas No. 6 and cook for a further 1 hour. Finally, open the foil so that the contents will be exposed directly to the heat. Sprinkle with parsley and increase the oven temperature to 475 deg. F or Gas No. 9 for final cooking time of 15–20 minutes. This last burst of heat is employed to produce a burnt effect which is associated with the smoky flavour, usually apparent in food cooked over open fires or by burial in and under a bonfire.

MONGOLIAN MEAT CAKES

Mongolian meat cakes from the Yuan Dynasty, A.D. 1274–1356 or earlier are rough-and-ready affairs with no pretensions to *haute cuisine* whatever. Quantities cooked at one time were very substantial and meat cakes would be about 1½ inches thick and 1 foot across. However, a more practical and civilized version of the recipe can be based on the following quantities.

1 lb lean lamb	*3 tablespoons butter or lard*
1 lb lamb's liver and kidney	*2 tablespoons soya sauce*
1 large onion	*2 tablespoons vinegar*
1¼ lb potatoes or yam	*4 tablespoons breadcrumbs*
2 slices root ginger	*4 tablespoons grated goat or cow's milk*
2 eggs	*cheese – use Cheddar or Parmesan*
4 level tablespoons cornflour	*2 level teaspoons sugar*
2 level teaspoons salt,	*2 tablespoons sesame seeds*
pepper to taste	*6 tablespoons sesame oil*

Trim and chop the lamb's meat, liver and kidney. Peel and chop the onion and potato and chop the ginger. Mix these together with the beaten eggs, cornflour, salt, pepper, butter or lard, soya sauce, vinegar, breadcrumbs, cheese and sugar. Mix the ingredients together thoroughly. Form the mixture into a 2–2½-inch-thick meat cake. Sprinkle the top of the meat cake with sesame seeds and press well into the cake with the palm or the hand or the fingers.

Heat some of the sesame oil in a very large flat frying-pan and tilt the pan so that the oil runs evenly over the surface. Place the meat cake gently in the pan. Fry over medium heat for 6–7 minutes. Spoon the remaining sesame oil evenly over the top of the meat cake. Place the frying-pan under a fairly hot grill for 6–7 minutes. Transfer the meat cake with the aid of two fish slices to a roasting tin. Set in a preheated oven (425 deg. F or Gas No. 7) and bake for 30–35 minutes.

To serve cut the 'cake' into slices, there should be sufficient for 5–6 portions. The blending of cheese, meats, onion, sesame oil and seeds should remind one of the flavours and aromas of the steppes of Central Asia.

TUNGPO PORK

This dish is believed to have been created by one of China's greatest poets, Su Tungpo, who lived from A.D. 1036 to 1101. He was always very much preoccupied with wine gastronomy, and is said to have created a good many dishes during the period when he was in exile.

2 lb belly of pork　　　　　　　　　*2 tablespoons soya sauce*
1½ level teaspoons salt　　　　　　　*4 tablespoons rice wine or dry sherry*
3 stalks of spring onions　　　　　　*1½ level teaspoons sugar*
2 slices of root ginger

Cut the pork through the skin into squares at 1-inch intervals. Sprinkle and rub the pork pieces with the salt and leave to season for 3 hours. Drain the pork from the extracted liquid and parboil the pieces in boiling water for 15 minutes. Pour away the water and parboil a second time in fresh boiling water for a further 15 minutes. Cut the spring onions into ½-inch segments. Shred the ginger.

Place and pack the pork pieces, skin side down, in a casserole. Mix the soya sauce, wine, sugar, spring onion segments and shredded ginger in a bowl. Sprinkle the mixture evenly over the pork. Bring the mixture to a simmer over direct heat, then cover with a tight-fitting lid and place the casserole in a slow oven (300 deg. F or Gas No. 2) and cook slowly for 2 hours.

Turn the pork out of the casserole into a deep-sided heatproof dish, skin side up. Cover the pork by wrapping in a piece of kitchen foil over the meat and dish. Place in a steamer and steam steadily for 1½ hours. Unwrap the tin foil and serve in the dish. The pork should be as tender as jelly.

WHITE COOKED PORK

Pork so cooked is prepared by subjecting the meat to a long period of simmering in water. The dish originated from the *Dawn* and *Dusk* sacrifices (as well as the *Sun* and *Moon* sacrifices) practised by the Manchurian court during the Ching Dynasty. A large well-selected pig was slaughtered and served up whole for the sacrifice. When the sacrifices were over the carcass was removed to the outhouse. There the court attendants along with the Imperial kitchen staff proceeded to develop three types of pork dishes and 'white cooked pork' is one of them. The tradition is now carried on by a well-known restaurant called Sha Kuo Chu in Peking, founded during the reign of Emperor Chien Lung. For preparing the dish any part of the pig can be used, except the head and trotters. For this recipe it is advisable to cook the pork in large quantities.

10 lb pork　　　　　　　　　　　*sesame seed hot cakes*

FOR THE DIPS
chopped garlic　　　　　　　　　*chilli sauce*
6–12 stalks spring onions　　　　*sesame seed oil*
soya sauce　　　　　　　　　　　*bean curd cheese*

Cut the pork into 6-inch-long and 3–4-inch-wide thick pieces. Place them in a heavy iron pot, saucepan or casserole. Cover with water and bring to the boil. Either place in a slow oven (300 deg. F or Gas No. 2) or set over direct heat with a simmering mat beneath for extra protection. Cook gently for 3 hours. It is important not to add any additional water once the cooking has started. After 30 minutes' cooking time, skim away all fat and impurities from the surface.

Crush and chop the garlic and cut the spring onions into $\frac{1}{2}$-inch segments. Place them on the table in separate dishes along with the soya sauce, chilli sauce, sesame seed oil and bean curd cheese, also in separate dishes. These are for the diners to select and mix into sauces of their own creation.

When the meat is ready, allow it to cool slightly. Slice the large chunks into smaller 3 by 3-inch pieces and serve. They should be eaten with toasted Peking hot cakes dipped first of all in the self-prepared dips. These hot cakes are made from ordinary flour with a small amount of baking powder, sugar and salt added. They are then covered on the outside with sesame seeds and cooked by heating on a griddle for 7–8 minutes. They can be further toasted just before serving.

MADAME WU'S PRESSED PIG'S HEAD AND KNUCKLE OF PORK

Madame Wu recommended many recipes which are surprisingly practical. This one gives evidence that the Chinese appreciation for fat and skin dates back at least to her time and probably long before.

1 pig's head	*4 pairs knuckle of pork*

FOR THE DIPS
soya sauce	*tomato sauce*
vinegar	

After removing all the hair from the pig's head and knuckles, place the items in a large cauldron and cover with water. Bring to the boil and simmer gently for $3\frac{1}{2}$–4 hours.

Remove the flesh from the head and knuckles – they should now be very easy to pick apart, and discard the bone. Wrap the skin, meat and tendons in a piece of clean cloth. Place the parcel in a colander and set a heavy weight on top. Leave to drain overnight.

Unwrap the parcel and cut the contents into neat pieces. Serve with the dips placed in small sauce dishes strategically arranged on the dinner-table.

QUICK-FRIED 'THREE PARTS OF LAMB'

This dish originated in Manchuria and was introduced into Peking during the Manchu Dynasty. A popular dish which can be had in most restaurants in China and occasionally abroad.

$\frac{3}{4}$ lb lean lamb	*3 stalks spring onions*
$\frac{1}{4}$ lb lamb's liver	*3 tablespoons sesame oil*
$\frac{1}{4}$ lb lamb's kidney	*$2\frac{1}{4}$ tablespoons soya sauce*
$1\frac{1}{2}$ level teaspoons salt	*1 tablespoon vinegar*
1 level tablespoon cornflour	*1 tablespoon rice wine or dry sherry*
2 cloves garlic	

Trim and dice the lamb's meat, liver and kidney into $\frac{1}{2}$-inch cubes. Sprinkle with the salt and cornflour and rub well in. Crush and chop the garlic. Cut the spring onion into $\frac{1}{2}$-inch segments.

Heat the sesame oil in a large frying-pan. When hot add the garlic and onion. Stir-fry quickly over high heat for $\frac{1}{2}$ minute. Add the lamb's meat, kidney and liver. Continue to stir-fry for 2 minutes. Add the soya sauce, vinegar and wine. Stir-fry for a further few minutes and serve hot.

Early American Recipes

These included some recipes using corn meal. This can be bought in Italian delicatessens under the Italian name *polenta*, but it is sold in many supermarkets.

POT LIKKER WITH CORN MEAL DODGERS

DUMPLINGS

If you are feeling cold and hard up there is nothing more heart-warming than this nourishing and economical dish which is full of down-to-earth country flavour. Served with bright yellow cornmeal dumplings, it conjures up a picture of the early settlers' kitchen and the women who knew how to make the best use of the simple ingredients to hand. The old recipe used turnip tops, but as these are seldom in the shops you will find that curly kale gives an equally good flavour.

SERVES 2–3
¼ *lb salt pork*
2½ *pints cold water*
salt and pepper

1¾ *lb turnip tops or curly kale*
    (to yield about 1 lb greens when picked over)

FOR THE CORN MEAL DUMPLINGS
2 *oz corn meal*
½ *level teaspoon salt*
2 *oz plain flour*

2 *oz melted butter*
water to mix – see recipe

Place the piece of pork in a saucepan and add the water. Bring to the boil, cover and simmer for 45 minutes. Add the greens and a seasoning of salt and pepper. Re-cover the pan and cook for a further 45 minutes.

About 10 minutes before the end of the cooking time prepare the corn meal dumplings. Mix the corn meal, salt and flour in a basin. Stir in the melted butter. Add 2–3 dessertspoons cold water and mix to a dough. Mould into small dumplings with lightly floured hands – makes 12 'dodgers'.

Dish the pot likker greens and the pork by tipping the liquor from the pan into a colander placed over a bowl. Lift out the pork and press the greens to remove excess liquid. Return the liquid to the saucepan and bring back to the boil. Gently drop in the corn meal dumplings. Cover and cook for 15–20 minutes.

Dice the pork and chop the greens. Keep hot in a warm earthenware dish. When the corn meal dumplings are cooked serve them round the edge of the dish with a good cupful of 'likker' from the pot poured over.

Southern Cook Book

277

SOUTHERN GUMBO

The word 'gumbo' is the Negro patois for the okra plant. It is now recognized as meaning a dish or soup thickened with okra. There are many types of gumbo, but all include okra which gives the flavour and texture to the dish.

SERVES 4

2 oz butter
1 large onion
1 large 10 or 12 oz tin okra, or
   ½ lb fresh okra
¾ lb tomatoes

1 large green pepper
1 pint water
salt and pepper
½ level teaspoon celery seed

Melt the butter in a large saucepan. Peel and finely chop the onion, add to the butter and fry gently until the onion is tender and beginning to brown.

Meanwhile drain the okra from the tin, or if using fresh okra remove the stalks and cap at the thick end. Scald the tomatoes and peel away the skins. Halve and de-seed the green pepper. Chop the okra, tomatoes and green pepper finely and then add to the onion in the pan. Stir in the water, a seasoning of salt and pepper and the celery seed. Simmer gently for 1 hour. Adjust seasoning and serve.

Southern Cook Book

EGGS NEW ORLEANS

This is a typical dish from New Orleans, which has both Spanish and French influences in its cooking.

SERVES 4

¾ lb tomatoes
1 small green pepper
1 small onion
1 large or 2 small sticks celery
bouquet garni – of 1 bay leaf, 2 sprigs thyme
   and 3 sprigs parsley tied in a bundle

salt and pepper
1 level teaspoon sugar
1 oz fresh white breadcrumbs
4 eggs
2 oz grated cheese

Scald the tomatoes and peel away the skins. Chop the tomato flesh coarsely and place in a saucepan. De-seed and chop the green pepper, peel and finely chop the onion and chop the celery. Add the vegetables to the pan along with a seasoning of salt and pepper, the bouquet garni and the sugar.

Set the pan over low heat and fry the vegetables gently together until sufficient juices run to prevent the vegetables sticking to the base of the pan. Cover the pan with a lid and simmer over lowest heat for 15–20 minutes, or until the vegetables are quite tender. Stir in the breadcrumbs and allow to cook for a further 2–3 minutes. Check seasoning and remove the bouquet garni.

Spoon the vegetable mixture into 4 individual ramekin dishes and make a depression in the top. Break an egg into each hollow and sprinkle over the grated cheese. Place in a moderate oven (350 deg. F or Gas No. 4) and bake for 10 minutes, or until the eggs have set and the cheese is melted.

Southern Cook Book

G'SHTUPTAFUL LEW'R

This Pennsylvania dish has an interesting link with a very early German recipe for stuffed liver which is almost identical. It was created by Max Rumpolt whose famous cookery book was published in 1604. When carved, the slices of pink liver look most attractive with alternate layers of green stuffing.

SERVES 4

1 whole lamb's liver
seasoned flour

½ pint chicken stock
3 thin strips salted belly of pork

FOR THE STUFFING

3 oz fresh white breadcrumbs
½ small onion, finely chopped
1 rounded tablespoon chopped parsley
1 level teaspoon salt
¼ level teaspoon ground pepper

pinch nutmeg
pinch allspice
pinch ground mace
2 tablespoons melted dripping
1 small egg

Wash and dry the liver. Set on a board round side up and using a sharp knife cut into the liver to form a pocket which will hold the stuffing. Set aside while preparing the stuffing mixture.

Place the breadcrumbs, chopped onion, chopped parsley, salt, pepper, nutmeg, allspice, and ground mace in a basin. Using a fork, stir in the melted dripping and lightly mixed egg. Mix to a moist but not wet consistency.

Pack the pocket in the liver with stuffing, but do not overfill. Turn the liver flat side up and pile some more of the stuffing on to the thick end. Flap over the thin end of the liver and the two little side flaps. Secure the neat shape of the stuffed liver with string, and dredge on both sides with seasoned flour. Place the liver in a roasting tin and add the stock – you may need more or less, according to the size of your roasting tin. The stock should come about ½ inch up the sides of the liver. Place the strips of pork fat over the liver to cover it completely. Set in a hot oven (450 deg. F or Gas No. 8) and cook for 15 minutes. Then reduce the heat to moderate (350 deg. F or Gas No. 4) and bake for a further 45 minutes.

When cooked remove any string and carve the liver in slices. The liquid in which the liver has cooked makes an excellent rich gravy to serve with it.

Traditional Pennsylvania Dutch

TEXAS ROUND-UPS

Served hot with grilled tomatoes or eaten cold, these Texas round-ups are delicious either way. They look attractive with the tasty filling speckled with green pepper and the pastry flecked with red pimento. They would make a good dish for an informal teenager party, or weekend lunch with cheese and beer. Fine for a picnic, too.

SERVES 6

1 lb lean steak
1 heaped dessertspoon finely chopped
  green pepper
1 heaped teaspoon finely chopped onion
1 level teaspoon salt

¼ level teaspoon ground pepper
1 teaspoon Worcestershire sauce
seasoned flour
butter for frying

8 oz plain flour
4 level teaspoons baking powder
1 level teaspoon salt

3 oz mixed butter and lard in equal proportions
2 heaped dessertspoons finely chopped pimento
scant ¼ pint milk

Mince the steak and place in a bowl. Add the green pepper, onion, salt, pepper and Worcestershire sauce. Handling the mixture lightly, shape into 8 small rolls and coat each one in seasoned flour. Fry in hot butter to seal and brown on all sides, then remove from the pan.

Sift the flour for the pastry, the baking powder and salt into a mixing bowl. Rub in the mixed fats and add the chopped pimento. Stir in the milk and mix with a fork to a rough dough. Turn out on to a floured surface and roll out thinly about ¼ inch thick. Cut into 8 equal rectangles.

Wrap each meat roll in a rectangle of pastry. Damp the edges and seal neatly. Place on a well-greased baking tin and set in a hot oven (450 deg. F or Gas No. 8) and bake for 15 minutes.

Western Cook Book

JAMBALAYAH

Rice combined with meat, fish or shellfish gives Jambalayah its distinctive flavour. A traditional Creole dish for which there are many variations. In this case it provides a savoury way of using up cooked chicken.

SERVES 4

8–12 oz cooked chicken flesh
5 tomatoes
1 small green pepper
1 medium onion
2 sticks celery

1½ teacups cooked rice
salt and pepper
stock or water – see recipe
2 oz fresh white breadcrumbs
½ oz butter

Dice the chicken flesh. Scald the tomatoes and peel away the skins. Halve and remove the seeds and then dice the tomato flesh. De-seed and chop the green pepper, slice the onion and celery thinly.

Place the chicken flesh, tomatoes, green pepper, onion, celery and cooked rice in a saucepan. Add a good seasoning of salt and pepper and pour in just sufficient stock or water to prevent the mixture from sticking to the base of the pan. Bring up to a simmer, cover and cook gently for about 15 minutes.

Turn the mixture into a buttered pie dish. Sprinkle with the breadcrumbs and dot generously with flakes of butter. Place above centre in a hot oven (400 deg. F or Gas No. 5) and bake for 30–40 minutes, until crumbs are crisp and golden brown.

Southern Cook Book

TAMALE PIE

A tasty layer of mince beef is spread between two layers of corn meal mush. The flavour has plenty of zest with the chilli powder and green pepper showing the Mexican influence on the cooking of the South-west.

SERVES 4

1¼ pints water
1½ level teaspoons salt
4 oz corn meal
2 oz black olives
1 medium onion

1 green pepper
4 tomatoes
2 oz butter
1 lb minced beef
1 level teaspoon chilli powder

Bring the water and 1 level teaspoon of the salt to the boil in a medium-sized saucepan. Stir in the corn meal, mixing well to get a smooth mixture. Cover the pan and leave to cook gently over a very low heat for 30 minutes, stirring occasionally. Stone the olives and cut into pieces, stir into the pan of corn meal, draw off the heat and allow to cool a little.

Meanwhile peel and chop the onion and de-seed and chop the green pepper. Scald the tomatoes, peel away the skins and chop the tomato flesh. Melt the butter in a large saucepan and add the onion. Cook gently for a few minutes until the onion is tender. Add the chopped green pepper and the minced beef. Stir over fairly high heat to brown the meat. Add the tomato flesh, chilli powder, the remaining ½ teaspoon of salt and draw off the heat.

Spoon half the corn meal mush into a buttered ovenproof dish. Spread the meat mixture over, and top with a final layer of corn meal mush. Dot with butter and place in the centre of a moderate oven (350 deg. F or Gas No. 4) and bake for 30 minutes.

Western Cook Book

DIXIE SHORTCAKE

Here is an unusual way of using up some cold chicken. Diced chicken and mushrooms in a creamy sauce is sandwiched between two layers of hot corn bread and topped with more of the chicken mixture. The corn bread has a good grainy texture and an attractive golden colour.

SERVES 4

FOR THE CORN BREAD

3 oz corn meal
3 oz plain flour
1 level teaspoon baking powder
¼ level teaspoon salt

1 egg
6 tablespoons milk
1 oz melted butter

FOR THE CHICKEN FILLING

1 lb cooked chicken flesh
¼ lb mushrooms
1 oz butter

1 rounded tablespoon flour
⅓ pint chicken stock
salt and pepper

Sift the corn meal, flour, baking powder and salt into a mixing basin. Lightly mix the egg and milk and stir into the dry ingredients. Add the melted butter and mix well to make a batter. Pour in a well-greased 7–8-inch, shallow, square baking tin. Set in a hot oven (425 deg. F or Gas No. 7) and bake for 30–35 minutes.

Meanwhile prepare the chicken filling. Remove any skin and dice the chicken flesh. Wipe and slice the mushrooms. Melt the butter in a saucepan and fry the mushrooms. Blend in the flour and then gradually add the chicken stock. Bring up to the boil, stirring all the time to thicken the sauce evenly. Season with salt and pepper, then add the diced chicken flesh and heat through gently.

Turn out the baked corn bread and when cool enough to handle, split in half lengthwise. Place one layer of corn bread on a shallow dish. Spoon over half the chicken filling. Cover with a second layer of corn bread and cut across into 4 portions. Pile the remaining chicken mixture on top and serve.

Southern Cook Book

SHNITZ UN KNEPP

This is a deliciously good way of cooking gammon with dried apple rings and dumplings. A recipe handed down from the Pennsylvanian German settlers.

SERVES 6, WITH COLD LEFT OVER
1 piece gammon, about 3 lb
3 oz dried apple rings, soaked overnight

1 rounded teaspoon demerara sugar

FOR THE DUMPLINGS
½ lb plain flour
½ level teaspoon baking powder
½ level teaspoon salt
¼ level teaspoon ground pepper

1 egg
2 oz melted butter
milk to mix – see recipe

Soak the gammon in cold water for several hours or overnight. Drain and place in a saucepan with fresh cold water to cover. Bring to the boil and simmer gently for 1 hour. Add the apple rings and the water in which they soaked, and the sugar. Simmer for a further 1 hour.

Meanwhile prepare the dumplings. Sift the flour, baking powder, salt and pepper into a mixing basin. Stir in the lightly mixed egg, the melted butter and sufficient milk to mix the ingredients to a soft dough. With floured hands roll portions of the dough into about 10 small dumplings.

Lift the gammon and apples from the pan on to a hot serving dish and keep warm. Bring the saucepan of liquid back to the boil and gently add the dumplings. Cover and simmer for 20 minutes. When cooked, drain from the liquor and serve with the gammon and apples.

Traditional Pennsylvania Dutch

WILD BLACKBERRY COBBLER

This is a deliciously unusual way of serving blackberries. The sweet batter crust goes beautifully with the rich bubbling blackberries underneath. Serve piping hot with chilled whipped cream when October evenings are drawing in and a seasonal hot pudding is welcome. Well-drained tinned, or frozen blackberries can be substituted, but lack that special zest of the wild berries.

SERVES 4

1 lb blackberries	1 teaspoon lemon juice
6 oz castor sugar	½ oz butter

FOR THE TOPPING

4 oz plain flour	2 oz castor sugar
2 level teaspoons baking powder	4 tablespoons milk
¼ level teaspoon salt	2 oz melted butter
1 egg	

Mix the blackberries with the sugar and lemon juice and place in a 1½ pint pie dish. Dot with flakes of the butter and set aside while preparing the topping.

Sift the flour, baking powder and salt on to a plate. Crack the egg into a mixing basin, add the sugar and beat well to mix. Stir in the milk and the melted butter. Gradually stir in the sifted flour mixture, beating very well all the time to get a smooth batter.

Pour the batter over the berries in the pie dish and spread level. Set in the centre of a moderate oven (350 deg. F or Gas No. 4) and bake for 30–35 minutes. Serve hot with cream.

Western Cook Book

STICKY CINNAMON BUNS

The Pennsylvanian settlers were famous for their home baking, and brought with them many delicious recipes like the one below.

MAKES ABOUT 12 BUNS

1 lb plain flour	2 oz melted butter
¼ level teaspoon salt	4 oz sultanas
7 oz soft brown sugar	2 oz currants
¼ pint mixed milk and water	4 oz chopped candied peel
1 level tablespoon dried yeast	2 level teaspoons ground cinnamon

Sift the flour and salt into a warm mixing basin. Mix in 3 tablespoons of sugar and set aside. Heat the liquid until a little hotter than lukewarm – about 110 deg. F or hand-hot. Stir in 1 teaspoon of the sugar and sprinkle in the yeast. Set aside in a warm place for about 10 minutes or until frothy.

Pour the yeast liquid into the centre of the dry ingredients and mix to a rough dough in the basin. Turn out and knead well for 10–15 minutes to make a smooth, soft dough. Place the dough in a greased basin, cover and leave in a warm place until well risen and double in size.

Turn the risen dough on to a floured working surface and press all over with the knuckles. Roll out to about ¼ inch in thickness and brush the surface all over with the melted butter. Mix together the sultanas, currants, chopped peel, cinnamon and 2 oz of the brown sugar. Sprinkle the fruit and sugar mixture over the surface of the dough. Starting at one end, roll the dough up like a Swiss roll. Cut in slices about ¾ inch thick. Place fairly close together in a well-buttered shallow baking tin. Sprinkle with the remaining brown sugar and leave in a warm place until puffy. Set in a hot oven (425 deg. F or Gas No. 7) and bake for 20–25 minutes.

Cool on a wire tray and pull the buns apart to serve.

Traditional Pennsylvania Dutch

LEBKUCHEN

This spice cake is of German origin and was probably first introduced to America through the kitchens of the Pennsylvania Dutch. The highly spiced flavour and very fruity texture of what is really more of a 'cookie' than a cake, quickly became popular. Now Lebkuchen is made in many American homes, particularly at Christmas. This recipe has a soft cake-like texture and like all recipes for Lebkuchen it keeps well.

CUTS INTO 3 DOZEN PIECES
10 oz plain flour
1 level teaspoon salt
1 level teaspoon baking powder
¼ level teaspoon ground cloves
1 level teaspoon ground cinnamon
1 level teaspoon allspice

3 large eggs
8 oz soft brown sugar
½ lb mixed glacé fruits such as cherries, candied peel and crystallized pineapple
4 oz walnuts, coarsely chopped
5 tablespoons strong black coffee or sherry

FOR THE ICING
4 oz icing sugar

juice of ½ lemon

Sift the flour, salt, baking powder and spices on to a plate. Crack the eggs into a warm mixing basin, add the sugar and whisk until thick and light. Fold in the sieved flour, the prepared glacé fruits, the walnuts and the coffee or sherry.

Pour the batter into a large shallow baking or roasting tin of approximately 14 by 10 inches; the batter should be about ½ inch thick. Place above centre in a moderately hot oven (375 deg. F or Gas No. 5) and bake for 25–30 minutes.

Sieve the icing sugar into a basin and stir in sufficient lemon juice to make a fairly stiff paste. Spread over the Lebkuchen while still warm and newly baked. Leave until cold and then cut in fingers.

Traditional Pennsylvania Dutch

284

CREOLE RICE CAKES

These can be served with a main course, taking the place of potato or rice. They go particularly well with grilled chops, liver or sausages, and look attractive with the speckles of green pepper and bacon in the faintly pink fritters, coloured with the fresh tomato pulp.

SERVES 4

4 oz long grain rice	*1 level teaspoon salt*
6 rashers streaky bacon	*½ level teaspoon ground pepper*
½ medium onion	*1 level teaspoon baking powder*
½ green pepper	*4 oz plain flour*
1 lb ripe tomatoes	

Add the rice to a saucepan of boiling salted water, cook for 12–14 minutes until tender, and drain well. Trim the bacon rashers and fry in a dry pan until the bacon fat runs and the rashers are crisp. Lift the bacon from the pan, reserve the bacon drippings and chop the rashers finely.

Place the rice in a bowl and add the chopped bacon. Peel and finely chop the onion and de-seed and chop the green pepper. Add both to the rice. Halve the tomatoes and press through a sieve to make about ½ pint tomato pulp. Discard skin and pips and add the tomato pulp to the rice along with the salt, pepper, baking powder and flour. Mix very thoroughly.

Reheat the bacon fat and add tablespoons of the mixture to the hot pan. When brown on one side, turn to cook the second side – from this mixture you should get about 12 pancakes. Add more bacon fat to the pan as necessary to fry all the rice cakes.

Southern Cook Book

SHOO-FLY PIE

This early American dish derives its picturesque name from the sweet ingredients which must have attracted swarms of flies in the old-fashioned kitchens. In spite of its sweetness, the molasses has a tang, and the pie remains crunchy and good if eaten hot or cold.

SERVES 6

4–6 oz shortcrust pastry	*3 tablespoons molasses or black treacle*
2 oz plain flour	*3 tablespoons hot water*
4 oz soft brown sugar	*¼ level teaspoon bicarbonate of soda*
4 oz butter	

Roll out the pastry and use to line an 8-inch pie plate. Trim edges and set aside while preparing the crumble topping.

Sift the flour into a mixing basin and add the sugar. Add the butter cut in pieces. Rub into the mixture until evenly blended and crumbly in texture.

Stir the molasses into the hot water, add the bicarbonate of soda and stir together until it fizzes. Cool for a few moments, then pour into the pastry-lined pie plate.

Scatter the crumble mixture thickly over the molasses. Set in a moderately hot oven (350 deg. F or Gas No. 4) and bake for 25 minutes, or until the crumble is firm. Serve hot or cold.

Traditional Pennsylvania Dutch

Index of Recipes